Volume **9** **THE**
GOLDEN BOOK
ENCYCLOPEDIA

hibernation to Ivory Coast

hi-iv

An exciting, up-to-date encyclopedia in 20 fact-filled, entertaining volumes

Especially designed as a first encyclopedia for today's grade-school children

More than 2,500 full-color photographs and illustrations

From the Publishers of Golden® Books

Western Publishing Company, Inc.
Racine, Wisconsin 53404

ILLUSTRATION CREDITS
(t=top, b=bottom, c=center, l=left, r=right)

1 l, Michael Adams/Publishers' Graphics; 1 r, Lloyd P. Birmingham; 3, Jeff Foott/Bruce Coleman Inc.; 4 bl, Brown Brothers; 4 br, from *A Guidebook of Mexican Coins* by T.V. Buttrey and Clyde Hubbard, © 1986, Western Publishing Company, Inc.; 5 tl, Jacques Jangoux/Peter Arnold, Inc.; 5 tr, © Joe Viesti; 6, Bettmann Archive; 7 t, John Henry Sullivan, Jr./Photo Researchers; 7 bl, David Lindroth Inc.; 8–9 b, Michael O'Reilly/Joseph, Mindlin & Mulvey; 10, Chris Bonington/Woodfin Camp; 11 bl, © Joe Viesti; 11 br, Art Resource; 11 inset, Scala/Art Resource; 12, Clem Haagner/ Bruce Coleman Inc.; 13 tl, Hiroshima Peace Memorial Museum; 13 tr, UPI/Bettmann Newsphotos; 14–15 b, David Rickman/Publishers' Graphics; 15 tl, Bettmann Archive; 16–17 t, Sandy Rabinowitz/Publishers' Graphics; 17 br, Benser/Zefa/H. Armstrong Roberts; 18, David Lindroth Inc.; 19 tl, Bruce Gordon/Photo Researchers; 19 tr, Jerry Cooke/Photo Researchers; 20 tr, Bettmann Archive; 20–21 b, Michael Adams/Publishers' Graphics; 22, George A. Gabriel; 23 b, Historical Picture Service, Chicago; 24, Winslow Homer, *The Herring Net,* 1885, oil on canvas, 74.3 x 120.2 cm, Mr. and Mrs. Martin A. Ryerson Collection, 1937.1039, © 1987 the Art Institute of Chicago, all rights reserved; 25, Gordon Wiltsie/Bruce Coleman Inc.; 26 tr, Transparency No. 649, Courtesy Department of Library Services, American Museum of Natural History; 26 bl, Jane Burton/Bruce Coleman Inc.; 27, Fiona Reid/Melissa Turk & The Artist Network; 28, Blair Seitz/Photo Researchers; 29 tl, Michal Heron/Woodfin Camp; 29 b, Tom Powers/ Joseph, Mindlin & Mulvey; 30, © Joe Viesti; 31 tl and 32 bl, David Lindroth Inc.; 32 c, Springer/Bettmann Film Archive; 33 and 34, Robert Frank/ Melissa Turk & The Artist Network; 36, Wayne Lankinen/Bruce Coleman Inc.; 37 cr, Adam Woolfitt/Woodfin Camp; 38, Allen Green/Photo Researchers; 39 t, NOAA; 39 inset, NASA; 40, Lloyd P. Birmingham; 41 tl, Arthur Sirdofsky; 42, Mimi Forsyth/Monkmeyer Press; 43, David Lindroth Inc.; 44, Wayne Lankinen/Bruce Coleman Inc.; 45 t, Francisco Erize/Bruce Coleman Inc.; 45 c, Dennis O'Brien/Joseph, Mindlin & Mulvey; 46 tl, Ben & Jerry's; 46 tr, American Dairy Association; 47 cr, Icelandair; 49 tl, Marilyn Bass; 49 c, David R. Frazier/Photo Researchers; 51 tl, Robert P. Carr/ Bruce Coleman Inc.; 51 cl, Marilyn Bass; 52, Brown Brothers; 53 t, David Lindroth Inc.; 53 br, © Joe Viesti; 54, Loren McIntyre/Woodfin Camp; 55 t inset, Loren McIntyre/Woodfin Camp; 55 br, Louis Goldman/Photo Researchers; 57 br, © Joe Viesti; 59 tl, Marilyn Bass; 59 c, Focus on Sports; 61, David Lindroth Inc.; 62–63 and 64–65, David Rickman/Publishers' Graphics; 66 tl, Dan Budnik/Woodfin Camp; 66–67, The Photo Source; 68 b, David Lindroth Inc.; 68 c, Bernard P. Wolff/Photo Researchers; 69, Gary Lippincott/Publishers' Graphics; 70 tl, Culver Pictures; 70 cr, Dr. D.J. McLaren/SPL/Photo Researchers; 71, Howard Sochurek/Woodfin Camp; 73 b, Dennis O'Brien/Joseph, Mindlin & Mulvey; 74, Wardene Weisser/ Bruce Coleman Inc.; 75 t, U.S. Department of Agriculture; 75 t inset, Lloyd P. Birmingham; 75 br, Marilyn Bass; 76, Lloyd P. Birmingham; 78–79 t, Gary Lippincott/Publishers' Graphics; 80 tr, Sepp Seitz/Woodfin Camp; 81 tr, Marilyn Bass; 82 bl, David Lindroth Inc.; 82 c, R.& S. Michaud/ Woodfin Camp; 83 tr, Homer Sykes/Woodfin Camp; 83 br, David Lindroth Inc.; 84 br, © Joe Viesti; 85, Brad Hamann; 86 b, Porterfield-Chickering/ Photo Researchers; 86 inset, Richard Hutchings; 87 both, Brown Brothers; 88 t, Marc & Evelyne Bernheim/Woodfin Camp; 88 inset, Lloyd P. Birmingham; 89 t, Robert Azzi/Woodfin Camp; 89 inset, © Joe Viesti; 90 b, Dennis O'Brien/Joseph, Mindlin & Mulvey; 91, David Lindroth Inc.; 92, Israel Government Tourist Office; 93 t, The Photo Source; 93 inset, David Lindroth Inc.; 94, NASA; 95 br, © Joe Viesti; 96, John Elk III/Bruce Coleman Inc.

COVER CREDITS
Center: Benser/Zefa/H. Armstrong Roberts. Clockwise from top: Art Resource; Fiona Reid/Melissa Turk & The Artist Network; Wayne Lankinen/ Bruce Coleman Inc.; Focus on Sports; David Rickman/Publishers' Graphics; Arthur Sirdofksy.

Library of Congress Catalog Card Number: 87-82741
ISBN: 0-307-70109-3

ABCDEFGHIJKLM

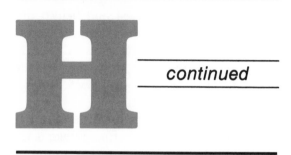

H *continued*

hibernation

In many parts of the world, it gets cold in winter. The temperatures fall below freezing. There is snow on the ground. Many animals that live in such areas spend the winters in caves, burrows, rocky crevices, and other protected places. They fall into a deep sleep that is called hibernation. Bats, groundhogs, and hamsters are some of the animals that hibernate.

During hibernation, an animal's breathing and other body processes slow down. A ground squirrel, for example, usually breathes about 200 times a minute. During hibernation, it breathes only two or three times a minute. The ground squirrel's heart usually beats about 400 times a minute. During hibernation, it beats only ten times a minute. The ground squirrel's body temperature falls to just above freezing while it is hibernating.

Even though the animal's body processes have slowed down, the animal still needs energy. In autumn, before the weather gets cold, the animal eats as much food as it can. Some of the food is turned into fat and stored in the body. This fat is used during hibernation to produce energy.

As winter ends, the days become warmer. The animal slowly comes out of hibernation. Its body processes speed up. Soon, it is wide awake. It leaves the den where it spent the winter and goes outside. It is much thinner in spring than it was at the beginning of winter. It is hungry and quickly starts to look for food.

Some animals seem to hibernate when the weather turns cold. Bears, skunks, and raccoons spend much of the winter sleeping, but they are not really hibernating. Their breathing and heartbeat slow down, but their temperatures do not fall. On a nice winter day, these animals may wake up. They go outside to look for food. Then they return to their dens and go back to sleep.

In some parts of the world, it gets very hot and dry in summer. In these places, mice and some other animals *estivate*. Estivation is very much like hibernation. All the body processes slow down. It almost seems as if the animal is dead. But when the environment improves, the animal becomes active again.

Certain frogs and fish estivate when their ponds dry up. Before the pond is completely dry, they bury themselves in mud. When rains fill the ponds with water, the frogs and fish begin to move about again. Some frogs do not even wait until the pond fills up. They come out when they hear raindrops falling on the dried mud above them.

A ground squirrel hibernates in its nest, sleeping through the winter.

Hidalgo y Costilla, Miguel

Miguel Hidalgo y Costilla started a movement in 1810 to make Mexico a free, self-governing country. He is known today as the "Father of Mexican Independence."

In the early 1800s, Mexico was a colony of Spain. Mexicans could not make their own laws. They could trade only with Spain. The most powerful government leaders were people born in Spain. Less important government jobs were sometimes held by *criollos* —people born in Mexico whose ancestors had come from Spain. The *mestizos*—people of mixed Spanish and Indian background—were farmers, craftsmen, and laborers. The Indians were very poor. They lived in their own villages or worked on plantations for wealthy landowners.

Hidalgo was a criollo, born in Mexico in 1753. He became a priest and helped the poor. At his church in the village of Dolores, he encouraged Indians to grow silkworms and to make bricks, pottery, and leather goods. It was against Spanish law for the Indians to make these things.

Hidalgo knew how the colonists in America had won independence from England. He felt the time had come for Mexico to follow this example and separate from Spain. In 1810, Hidalgo saw his chance. France had invaded Spain in 1808, and the Spanish were still fighting the French. Spanish rule had grown weak in Mexico. Hidalgo plotted a revolt.

At midnight on September 15, 1810, Hidalgo was awakened with the news that the Spanish had learned of his plan. He decided he must act quickly. He rang the church bell to call the Indians and mestizos. He made a moving speech to them and cried out for Mexican independence. Hidalgo's speech became known as the *grito de Dolores*—the "cry of Dolores."

Hidalgo led an untrained army of about 50,000 Mexicans to Mexico City, the capital. His army won many battles along the way. But in 1811, the strong Spanish troops captured and killed Hidalgo. Mexico finally won its independence from Spain in 1821.

Every year, Mexico honors Hidalgo. On September 15, the president of Mexico rings a bell in memory of Hidalgo and his *grito de Dolores*. Mexicans celebrate September 16 as Independence Day.

See also **Mexico.**

Hidalgo (left) fought to make Mexico an independent country. His picture appears on Mexican coins.

Two ancient kinds of picture writing. At left are hieroglyphs in stone made by the Maya in Central America. At right are Egyptian hieroglyphs in clay.

hieroglyphics

Hieroglyphics are a kind of picture writing. The word *hieroglyphic* means "sacred carving." At first, we used the word only for the writing of ancient Egyptians. Today, we often use it as a name for other picture writing as well.

Each picture is called a *hieroglyph.* Hieroglyphs that stand for ideas or things are called *ideograms.* For example, the ideogram for "man" is a picture of a man. Later, some hieroglyphs came to stand for sounds. In Egyptian hieroglyphics, a drawing of an owl often represents the sound *m.* This is because the Egyptian word for "owl" had an *m* sound. Some hieroglyphs stand for syllables or groups of consonant sounds. So one hieroglyph may stand for several words that have the same consonants but different vowels.

The earliest Egyptian hieroglyphics were carved in stone around 3100 B.C. These early hieroglyphics were ideograms. Later, ideograms and sound hieroglyphs were used together. Writing usually went from right to left. Sometimes it went from left to right, or top to bottom. A person could tell which way to read horizontal writing by looking at the pictures of people and animals. They all faced the beginning of the line.

Besides carving hieroglyphics in stone, the Egyptians wrote with pen and ink on *papyrus*—a kind of early paper. They made the pictures simpler by using a flowing, cursive writing called *hieratic.* Over the years, the cursive writing looked less and less like pictures. It turned into an even simpler writing style called *demotic.* Most people who used demotic writing could not read the earliest hieroglyphics. After a while, even the demotic hieroglyphics were not used. An alphabet replaced them.

By the year A.D. 300, no one could read the hieroglyphics. People did not know that some hieroglyphs stood for sounds and others for ideas. In 1799, a stone was found in Rosetta, Egypt. On the stone were three kinds of writing—old hieroglyphics, demotic hieroglyphics, and Greek. By 1832, Jean-Francois Champollion, of France, had figured out how to read Egyptian hieroglyphics by studying the Rosetta stone.

Other ancient people had systems of hieroglyphics, often called *glyphs.* The Hittites of ancient Turkey and the Minoans of the island of Crete used glyphs. The Maya in Central America and the Aztec in what is now Mexico used picture writing, too. People today are beginning to understand these writing systems.

See also **writing** and **alphabet.**

5

highway

Highways are important roads between cities. In the United States, giant highways called *interstate highways* crisscross the country in every direction. Nearly everyone who travels by car or bus uses the interstates, because travel on them is fast and safe. Trucks carry all kinds of freight on the highways, too. They carry everything from chickens and milk to new cars and giant machines. Sometimes, people even move houses on the highways.

Highway History Today's highways are among the best ever built. The U.S. highway system is also the largest system ever made. In the days before automobiles, there were very few highways. What people called "highways" back then would be considered dangerous back roads now.

In ancient times, people looking for food and water followed trails or paths made by animals. They made the trails easier to follow by removing rocks and trees. About 3500 B.C., the wheel was invented. Better roads were built for carts and wagons.

The Romans were the first great road builders. Nearly 2,000 years ago, they put together a whole system of highways to connect their large empire. With good roads, traders from one part of the empire could take goods to other parts. In case of trouble, the Roman government could use the roads to move armies.

Roman roads were much like modern highways. The workmen used stone blocks and gravel held together with cement. Some Roman roads were so well built that parts of them still can be seen today.

The roads in early America were used by horse-drawn wagons and carriages, and by people walking from place to place. Most roads were made of dirt. In rainy weather and in the spring when the snow melted, they became very muddy. In the winter, the ruts froze hard. They could trip horses and break carriage wheels. In many places, travel was possible only in summer and fall.

Workers lay down logs to form a bumpy *corduroy* road in the 1800s.

Even in good weather, the highways were bumpy and travel was slow. One large highway was the Boston Post Road. It ran from New York City to Boston, a distance of 200 miles. A trip between the two cities took about two weeks! Carriages traveled only during the day and covered less than 15 miles on an average day. A horseman could travel faster and might reach Boston in only a week.

In the early 1800s, John McAdam, a Scotsman, invented a new way to build paved roads. He decided that a stone base was unnecessary. Instead, he packed and leveled soil to support the weight of traffic. On top of the soil, he packed thin layers of crushed rock. Macadam pavement provided a smooth surface and kept the underlying soil dry.

By 1900, some main roads in cities were paved. But most highways between towns were still made of dirt. The invention of the automobile made better roads necessary.

Highways Today Today's highway builders often use concrete to build major highways. Interstate highways have overpasses and underpasses so that traffic does not have to stop at intersections. This makes travel both faster and safer. Interstates also climb hills gradually and turn corners very gently.

Interstate highways are designed to make travel fast and safe. They have no sharp curves or steep hills, and have "cloverleaf" interchanges instead of intersections.

Highway builders use explosives and modern earth-moving equipment to blast hills and mountains out of the way. Drivers on the new highway will have a smooth, easy trip. To make travel even more pleasant, some highways have rest areas, spots with picnic tables, and places to stop and enjoy the scenery along the way.

In all, there are about 41,000 miles of interstate highways in the United States. If you could straighten them out into one long line, they would go nearly twice around the world!

Numbering Highways The planners of the interstate highways in the United States gave each interstate highway a different number. The number tells something about the highway's direction and what part of the country it passes through.

Interstate highways that go north and south all have *odd numbers,* starting with 5 and ending with 95. Interstate 5 travels near the Pacific coast from southern California to Washington. Interstate 95 travels near the Atlantic coast from Florida to Maine.

Interstate highways that go east and west have *even numbers,* starting with 10 and ending with 90. Interstate 10 goes from southern California to Florida. Interstate 90 travels from Washington State in the west to Massachusetts in the east.

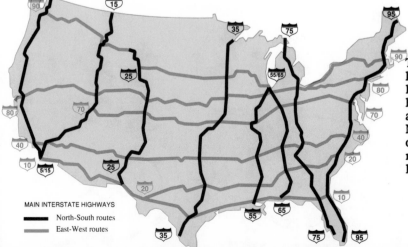

This map shows main interstate highways. East-west routes have even numbers, with the lowest numbers in the South and the highest in the North. North-south routes have odd numbers, with the lowest numbers in the West and the highest in the East.

MAIN INTERSTATE HIGHWAYS

North-South routes

East-West routes

Highway Safety In some ways, highways are much safer today than they have ever been. There are fewer accidents per mile traveled than there were in 1920. But because so many people travel and cover so many miles in a short time, highway accidents are a serious problem. In the United States, traffic accidents kill more than 40,000 people each year.

Highway planners keep working to design safer highways. Still, people must learn to obey speed limits and drive more safely. Even on the best roads, careless driving will cause accidents.

hiking

Millions of people enjoy taking long walks through parks and forests. This popular form of exercise is called hiking. Many people hike to look at beautiful scenery and see different kinds of animals and plants. Others hike because they like to exercise in fresh air and pleasant surroundings. A hike can last for an hour, a few days, or longer. An experienced hiker can travel more than 10 miles (16 kilometers) a day.

Not much equipment is needed for a short hike. The most important thing for a hiker to have is a comfortable pair of boots or shoes. It is also helpful to wear rugged clothing, such as jeans. In warm weather, hikers may wear shorts. Weather can change very quickly, so experienced hikers often take along more than one layer of clothing. Then they can put on or remove a layer to stay warm or cool off.

For long trips, hikers carry their equipment on their backs in *backpacks*. These have metal frames that help support the weight of the pack and make it easier to carry.

Hikes that last overnight or several days take planning and equipment. Hikers must bring everything they will need—food, clothes, and shelter—with them. But they also want to keep their backpacks as light as possible. Good tents and sleeping bags are usually made of lightweight, waterproof materials. For longer trips, many experienced hikers bring *dehydrated* foods. These are meats, vegetables, and fruits from which the water has been removed. Removing the water makes the food much lighter.

Backpackers carry all their supplies with them, including dried foods and lightweight sleeping bags. The hiker at left has a telescoping pole for fishing.

Water can be added later, during cooking. Smart hikers avoid packing any kind of heavy containers, such as glass jars. An experienced hiker can stay out on the trail for a week with just 15 pounds of supplies.

Many hiking areas and parks have maps showing trails. It is always best to keep to these trails. A map and compass can be a big help on any hike. A compass tells you in which direction you are headed. This can keep you from getting lost, and so every hiker should carry one.

One of the most famous hiking trails in the United States is the Appalachian Trail. This long trail runs from Maine to Georgia—a distance of about 2,000 miles (3,218 kilometers). The Pacific Crest Trail extends for more than 2,000 miles (3,218 kilometers) along the western coast of the United States.

Himalayas

The Himalaya Mountain System, which is in south-central Asia, is the highest in the world. A mountain system is made up of several mountain ranges. Twenty-nine of the peaks in the Himalayas soar 25,000 feet (7,600 meters) or more above sea level. One of them, Mount Everest, is the world's tallest mountain. It rises 29,028 feet (8,848 meters). (*See* **Everest, Mount.**)

Above 15,000 feet (4,600 meters), the mountains are almost completely covered with snow all year. The name *Himalaya* means "House of Snow." Some people believe that a creature called the Abominable Snowman, or *yeti*, lives in the Himalayas. Yeti is supposed to have the face of a human and the body of a giant, hairy ape. But no one has proved that the creature exists.

The Himalayas curve across northern Pakistan and India, and southern Tibet. They cover the kingdoms of Nepal and Bhutan. The system is about 1,500 miles (2,414 kilometers) long. Its width is between 125 and 200 miles (201 to 322 kilometers).

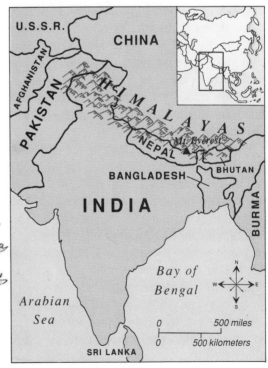

A farmer plows a field in the Himalayan foothills of Pakistan.

Many glaciers flow down the mountain slopes. These rivers of ice melt as they reach lower heights. This water is the source of southern Asia's important rivers—the Indus, Ganges, and Brahmaputra. (*See* glacier.)

Very few people live in the Himalayas. They make their homes in the mountain valleys or on the lower slopes. They work as farmers or herders. The farmers grow rice, corn, wheat, barley, and other crops. The herders look after sheep, goats, and yaks. The yak—a long-haired ox—is very important to the people of Nepal and Bhutan. It provides milk and meat. Its furry skin is used for warm clothing. The yak is also a sturdy work animal.

Perhaps the best-known people living in the Himalayas are the Sherpa. These people are skilled mountain climbers. They act as guides and porters for climbers of Everest and other mountains in the region.

It is not cold in all parts of the Himalayas. In some of the lower valleys, the summers are hot and winters are mild. Rare and endangered leopards and tigers live here, along with bears and other animals. Above 15,000 feet (4,600 meters), there are few animals. At this height, the temperature is rarely above freezing.

Hinduism

Hinduism is the major religion of India. A person who follows this religion is called a *Hindu.* There are more than 500 million Hindus. Most of them live in India, but there are Hindus in many other nations, including England and the United States.

Hindus believe there is one everlasting spirit, called *Brahma.* Hindus say that Brahma is everywhere and in everything in the world. Some Hindus believe only in Brahma, but most believe there are many gods. They see these different gods as parts of Brahma. Hindus place colorful images of these gods in their homes and temples.

Five gods are especially important to Hindus. Shiva is the god who makes and destroys things. Vishnu is the god who protects and preserves things. Vishnu is also called Rama and Krishna.

Shakti is called the "universal mother." She is a very powerful goddess. Surya is the sun god. The god Ganesha has the head of an elephant. Hindus believe that Ganesha lives in those places where two roads cross, or on the tops of hills.

Hindus believe that after a person dies, he or she will return to life again as a different person or even as an animal or an insect. The English word for this idea is *reincarnation.* Hindus believe that people are reborn—reincarnated—over and over again. What a person does in one life determines what his or her next life will be. This is called a person's *karma.* People may free themselves from this birth-death-rebirth cycle by living good lives, studying their religion, and honoring the gods and ancestors.

Hindu beliefs are written down in several books. The oldest Hindu scriptures are the Vedas, collections of songs and teachings. The words of religious leaders are collected in the Upanishads. Books called Dharma Sastras describe the ways people should live. Stories about gods and heroes are known as Puranas. Hindu religious books are written in the Sanskrit language.

The most important place for Hindu prayer and worship is at home with the family. The Hindu family includes not only the people who live together in a house but also their ancestors. Hindu families keep a small shrine in their homes. At the beginning and end of each day, they gather at the shrine for prayers. They offer food and flowers to their ancestors and to the gods. Hindus believe that their families are watched over by Agni, the god who protects Hindu homes.

Hindus have a great respect for all living things—for other people, and for animals, birds, insects, and plants. This respect for life is called *ahimsā.* Many Hindus are vegetarians, which means they do not eat any meat. They consider the lives of cows especially sacred. Most Hindus will not eat beef, no matter how hungry they may be.

Hindus must give something each day to their gods, their religious leaders, their ancestors, poor people, and animals. This is one way a person lives a good Hindu life.

Hindus believe that everyone is born into the world with an assigned role, called a *caste.* People must do what is expected of their castes. This duty is called their *dharma.*

Some Hindus practice *yoga,* a way of controlling and calming the body and mind. Hindus believe that a person who practices yoga will be strong and healthy in both body and spirit.

In the Hindu home, each important change in a person's life is greeted with special prayers and rituals. There is a great religious celebration when a baby is born. There

Hindus make statues of their many gods and goddesses. The goddess at right has four arms.
Below right, a Hindu temple built in the 1200s. Hindus visit a temple to meditate by themselves and to visit the gods. They do not have services of worship.
Below left, faithful Hindus bathe in the sacred Ganges River in the city of Benares. Many travel hundreds of miles to reach the holy waters of the river.

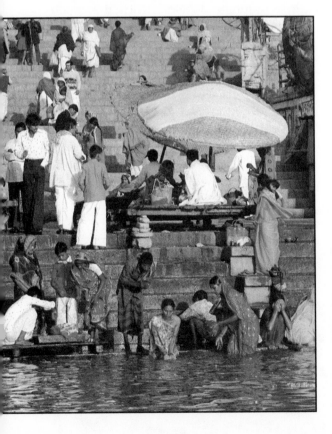

is another celebration when the baby eats solid food for the first time. A young person going away to school is sent off with special prayers by the family.

Sometimes Hindus worship in temples called *mandirs,* where they pray before a sacred flame. They also make special trips to the holy city of Benares so they can bathe in the Ganges River. Hindus believe that the Ganges has powers to heal and purify them spiritually.

hippopotamus

The hippopotamus, or "hippo," is a large African mammal. It has a big head, short legs, and a body shaped like a barrel. Hippos look clumsy, but they can move very quickly if they have to. A hippo can run faster than a human being!

The common hippo spends most of its life in water. The nostrils, eyes, and ears are on top of the head. This allows a hippo to breathe and keep track of what is happening in the environment while almost its entire body is under water. When a hippo wants to go completely under water, it can close its nostrils. It can stay under water for five minutes or more before it has to go back to the surface to breathe.

A hippo has two huge *tusks* in its lower jaw. The tusks are actually two canine teeth that never stop growing. The tusks are very sharp. When a hippo fights, it slashes its enemy with its tusks.

Hippos spend the daytime in water. At night, they go onto land to feed. They walk along trails they have made by trampling down plants. Each night, a hippo eats about 40 kilograms (88 pounds) of grass.

Hippos gather in groups called *schools.* Usually, there are about ten hippos in a school, but some schools may contain more than 100 hippos. A school consists of females, babies, and young hippos. Adult males live alone, though they usually stay close to a school.

Male hippos may be more than 4.25 meters (14 feet) in length and weigh more than 3,200 kilograms (3.5 tons). Female hippos are smaller. The females give birth on land or in shallow water. The babies weigh about 42 kilograms (93 pounds). They look like pigs. They can swim before they can walk. Mother hippos take good care of their babies. They try to protect them against crocodiles and lions, which are always on the lookout for unprotected young hippos.

A second kind of hippo is the pigmy hippo. It lives in jungles in West Africa. It is much smaller than the common hippo. Unlike the common hippo, it usually lives alone or in pairs. Also, it spends more time on land than the common hippo does.

People are the worst enemies of hippos. People hunt hippos for their meat and tusks. As people build farms and roads, they destroy the hippos' homes. The hippos have nowhere to live or find food. Today, hippos are scarce except in national parks.

A school of hippos crosses a shallow stream in Africa. They spend most of the day in the water to keep cool. At night, they come up on land to eat grass.

In August 1945, the atomic bomb destroyed most of Hiroshima and killed more than 75,000. The photos show part of the city before the blast and afterward.

Hiroshima

Hiroshima, a city in Japan, was the first city in the world to be destroyed by an atomic bomb. This happened toward the end of World War II, in 1945. Until then, atomic weapons had never been used in a war. The United States hoped that the Japanese would quickly surrender when they saw what this new weapon could do.

Before the attack occurred, Hiroshima was an important Japanese military and industrial center. On August 6, 1945, a U.S. plane flew over Hiroshima and dropped an atomic bomb near the center of the city. At least 75,000 people were killed instantly, and thousands died later from the effects of radiation. Almost all of Hiroshima's buildings were destroyed. A few days later, the United States dropped a second atomic bomb, on the city of Nagasaki.

The bombings of Hiroshima and Nagasaki brought a quick end to the war with Japan. But many people believe the war would have ended soon anyway, and that killing civilians was wrong. Others say thousands of soldiers on both sides would have died if the war had continued.

Hiroshima has since been rebuilt, and has more than twice as many people than it had in 1945. But the suffering caused by the atomic bomb will not be forgotten by the world. Visitors to Hiroshima can view the Memorial Shrine and the Atomic Age Museum and Exposition Center. It was built after the war in memory of the victims and to promote peace.

See also **World War II.**

history

History is a branch of knowledge that deals with the human past. *Historians*—experts in history—study the events of earlier times. They try to figure out why things happened as they did. They write about the past and teach other people about it. In a way, we are all historians. For example, when your grandparents tell you how they met, or talk about their wedding, they are telling you the history of your family.

A historian usually studies one particular country, time period, event, or person. For example, many historians have studied Christopher Columbus and his voyages in the late 1400s. Others have studied the events that led to the U.S. Civil War.

Historians use every kind of record in their studies. They look at the pictures carved on ancient city walls. Such pictures may tell about a brave ruler's deeds. Pictures on coins and pottery also give information about the past. But the most important tools for the historian are written records. For this reason, the time before people learned to write is called *prehistory*. (*Pre-* comes from a Latin word meaning "before.")

Written records include newspapers, letters, diaries, government records, and even lists kept by merchants. Historians also study folktales, folk songs, and books by earlier historians. They may watch videotapes or films, examine photographs and artwork, or talk to people about their experiences.

The historian's job is like doing a jigsaw puzzle. After studying the pieces, the historian puts them together so they make a "picture." For example, a historian might want to learn about American women pilots in World War II. He or she would read books and magazine and newspaper articles about the women pilots. The women's letters and diaries would be studied. The historian might talk to the women and check government records. After collecting all this information, the historian would organize the facts and write about what he or she had found.

The Greeks were the first people to write history that was based on firsthand experience instead of on stories and legends. For a long time, historians wrote mainly about rulers and wars. Now, they also try to understand what everyday life was like for ordinary people.

AGES OF HISTORY

Ancient Times
2000 B.C.-A.D. 500

Middle Ages
500-1200

Renaissance
1200-1700

Hitler, who began World War II, was one of history's most evil leaders.

Hitler, Adolf

Adolf Hitler ruled Germany from 1933 to 1945. More than any single person, he brought on World War II. He was responsible for enormous destruction and for the deaths of millions of people.

Hitler was born in 1889 in Austria. As a young man, he moved to Germany. Jobs were scarce, so he volunteered to serve in the army. In war, he found a purpose for his life. He won honors for bravery and learned to use violence to get what he wanted.

Hitler built up a political party called the Nazis. He attracted large crowds with powerful speeches. His Nazi party tried to seize power in 1923, but failed. Hitler was sent to jail. While there, he wrote a book called *Mein Kampf*—"My Struggle." In it, he described the Germans as a "master race" that should rule all others. Hitler was an *anti-Semite*—a person who hates Jews. He blamed the Jews for Germany's problems.

When he got out of jail, Hitler again tried to take over the government—legally, this time. The German government was weak. The country was suffering from its defeat in World War I and from the effects of the Great Depression. (*See* **depression.**)

Hitler promised to restore Germany to glory. By 1933, he was in power. As dictator, he completely controlled the police and the army. He built Germany's armed forces into a war machine and invaded Austria and Czechoslovakia. His invasion of Poland, in 1939, started World War II. Britain and France had promised to defend Poland, and they declared war on Germany.

At first, Germany won many battles. But then Germany tried to invade the Soviet Union. Hitler could not defeat the Soviet army, but he refused to admit it. He also did not realize how much stronger his enemies would be when the United States entered the war on their side.

Hitler fought the war to gain control of a huge territory, and to put his ideas of a "master race" into practice. The Germans forced thousands of Polish and Russian prisoners to do hard labor, and many died. For the Jews, Hitler planned what he called the "final solution"—death. The Nazis brought Jews from all over Europe to special camps. Almost 6 million Jews were killed in these camps. Another 6 million Europeans died in camps and from forced labor.

When Soviet, U.S., and other Allied forces began closing in on Germany, Hitler hid in an underground room. Early in 1945, he committed suicide.

See also **World War II.**

Modern Times
1700-present

Here are some of the activities that can become entertaining hobbies—birdwatching, baking, jogging, building dinosaur models, solving puzzles, and collecting posters.

hobby

A hobby is something a person does for fun in his or her spare time. People take up hobbies to relax and to learn things, too. Almost any activity can become a hobby. Some people enjoy gardening or playing a musical instrument or dancing. Other people collect rocks or watch the stars.

There are four main kinds of hobbies—collecting things, making things, playing or watching sports or games, and learning how to do something. Many hobbies combine two or more of these activities.

Collecting is one of the easiest hobbies. Coins, stamps, seashells, and matchbooks are among the most popular items that people collect. Other people collect more unusual objects, such as old woodworking tools or lace. Records, baseball cards, and insects make good collections, too. People who collect similar things like to trade with each other, to build up their collections.

Many people make things as a hobby. They like working with their hands and seeing the things they are making take shape. Some people hook rugs, knit, crochet, or design and sew their own clothes. Others build furniture or create sculptures. Do-it-yourself kits come with all the parts and instructions needed to put together things such as model cars and airplanes. Some people make cooking their hobby.

People of all ages enjoy sports and games as hobbies. Golf, tennis, baseball, and bowling are all popular. Many people make a hobby out of watching a certain sport and studying its rules and history. People relax

The choice of a hobby also depends on how much time and money a person can give to it. Some hobbies, like raising pets, may take an hour or more of a person's time every day. People who collect old cars spend a lot of money on their collections. Even children who collect baseball cards must spend money on their collections. Making things can be expensive, too, if special tools and materials are needed.

Once you have chosen a hobby, you will probably want more information about it. You may want a teacher or coach who can help you develop skills needed for your hobby. Joining a club is one way to find out more about your hobby. Club members share information and equipment. Many schools and collectors have clubs. Organizations such as the Scouts have activities and information about hobbies.

A hobby can lead to a career or remain a life-long interest. Many famous authors started writing as a hobby. Some hobbies can make money. A collection can become valuable. Rare baseball cards, for example, can be worth hundreds or even thousands of dollars. People who make things often sell what they make. For most people, however, a hobby is simply a way to have fun.

See also **collecting.**

by playing chess and card games, and by doing crossword or jigsaw puzzles.

Learning to do something well is one reason people take up certain hobbies. Watercolor painting, singing, and tumbling are more fun when they are done skillfully. But it takes practice to become good at these activities. Just learning about something can also be a hobby. People study history, literature, and music. They may learn as much as they can about a famous person or event.

Most people choose a hobby simply because it is something they like to do. They may enjoy ice-skating, making ice cream with different flavors, or turning metal into jewelry. Many people take up a hobby to develop a natural talent. For example, someone who sings well might join a chorus or take voice lessons.

Building models of ships and airplanes is a popular craft hobby.

hockey

Hockey is a team sport. Players use long, curved wooden sticks to hit an object into their opponents' goal. The word *hockey* probably comes from the French word *hoquet,* the name for a shepherd's crook.

Ice Hockey Ice hockey is played on ice skates on an ice rink. Most rinks are about 200 feet (61 meters) long and 85 feet (26 meters) wide. At each end of the rink is a *goal line.* In the middle of each goal line stands a *goal cage.* Two teams with six players each compete. The players use their sticks to pass a hard rubber disk, called a *puck,* along the ice. A team scores when the puck crosses the goal line and enters the opponents' goal cage.

Ice hockey began in Canada around the middle of the 1800s. The game soon spread to the United States and Europe. In 1917, the National Hockey League (NHL) was formed. NHL teams are made up of professional hockey players who represent cities in Canada and the United States. Ice hockey became an Olympic sport in 1920.

Ice hockey is a fast, exciting game. The puck may skid over the ice as fast as 100 miles (160 kilometers) per hour. Skaters must change direction quickly. Many of the NHL's best skaters are from Canada. (*See* **Gretzky, Wayne.**)

Other good players have come from Sweden, Finland, the United States, and the Soviet Union. Since 1960, Soviet teams have won more Olympic medals and world hockey titles than any other country.

Field Hockey Field hockey is played on a grass field 100 yards (91.4 meters) long and 60 yards (55 meters) wide. A goal cage is at each end. Each team has 11 players. They use wooden sticks, similar to those used in ice hockey, to hit a small rubber ball into the opposing team's goal cage. In field hockey, the players do a great deal of running.

Field hockey has been played in England for hundreds of years. It was first played in the United States in the early 1900s. In the United States today, field hockey is a popular sport for women. In many other countries, men and women play. Men's and women's teams compete in the Olympics.

In ice hockey, a team has two defensemen, three forwards, and a goalie. One team tries to put the puck into the other team's goal.

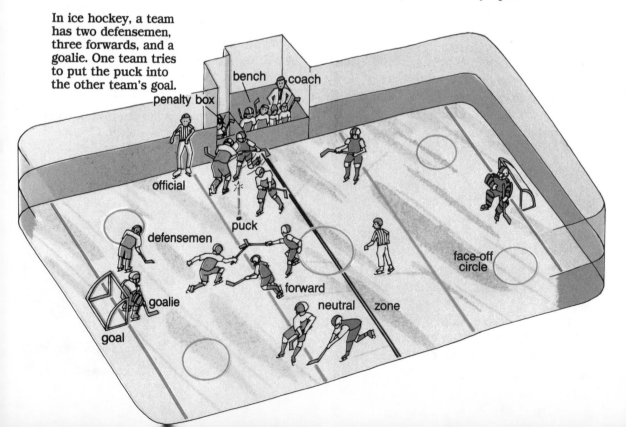

bench
coach
penalty box
official
puck
defensemen
forward
goalie
goal
neutral zone
face-off circle

At left, a shopkeeper in India sells candles for use at the feast of Dewali.
At right, Americans celebrate New Year's Day at California's Rose Parade.

holiday

A holiday is a day we set aside for a celebration. The word *holiday* comes from the words *holy day.* The first holidays were for religious celebrations. Holidays also honor people or events.

Religious Holidays Each religion has holidays to remember important events. To Christians, the birth of Jesus Christ is very important. It is celebrated at Christmas. Christians believe that Jesus came back to life after he had been dead for three days. They celebrate this event at Easter. Jews celebrate their escape from slavery in Egypt with the holiday of Passover. Muslims remember the birth of Muhammad, and Buddhists celebrate the birth of Buddha. Hindus in India honor Lakshmi, the goddess of wealth and good luck, during a fall festival called Dewali. (*See* **Christmas; Easter;** and **Passover.**)

Halloween and Valentine's Day began as religious holidays. But today they are celebrated as days for fun. (*See* **Halloween** and **Valentine's Day.**)

National Holidays Each nation has holidays to celebrate events important to its history. The date a country became an independent nation is usually a holiday. In the United States, this is celebrated on the Fourth of July, the date the Declaration of Independence was signed. Canada celebrates Canada Day on July 1, the date the first four provinces united in 1867. The Soviet Union celebrates the start of the Russian Revolution. Countries also set aside days to honor their soldiers and important leaders. Many national holidays are celebrated with parades and speeches. (*See* **Fourth of July.**)

Legal Holidays A legal holiday is a day set aside by a nation or state. On a legal holiday, schools, banks, libraries, and federal or state offices are closed. In the United States, on a federal legal holiday, people who work for the federal government or in the District of Columbia do not have to go to work.

Each state decides which days will be its own legal holidays. Some states do not observe all the federal legal holidays. Many states have a holiday on Abraham Lincoln's birthday, Good Friday, and Election Day.

Some people must still work on legal holidays. Many bus and train drivers work. Police officers, fire fighters, nurses, and doctors also work. Many people have jobs that need to be done all day, every day.

See also **Arbor Day; Thanksgiving; Labor Day; Yom Kippur; Memorial Day;** and **New Year's Day.**

U.S. LEGAL HOLIDAYS

New Year's Day	January 1
Martin Luther King, Jr., Day	the third Monday in January
Presidents' Day	the third Monday in February
Memorial Day	the last Monday in May
Independence Day	July 4
Labor Day	the first Monday in September
Columbus Day	the second Monday in October
Veterans Day	November 11
Thanksgiving	the fourth Thursday in November
Christmas Day	December 25

Holland, *see* **Netherlands, The**

Holmes, Sherlock

Sherlock Holmes is the name of a famous detective. But he never really lived, except in books. He is a character created by Sir Arthur Conan Doyle. Doyle wrote 56 short stories and four novels about Holmes. The first novel, *A Study in Scarlet,* appeared in 1887.

Holmes became famous for solving mysteries and crimes that no one else could figure out. He solved the mysteries by thinking about how all the details fit together. He had a sharp eye for details. He saw footprints left in a carpet. He saw what kind of cigar ash was dropped. He studied people's clothes and hands. He knew all about guns, knives, paper, ink, and medicines. He also had a perfect memory. He could remember what the weather was like on the day the crime happened. Holmes played the violin to help him

Sherlock Holmes used a magnifying glass and other tools to look for scientific clues.

think. His friend, Dr. Watson, was always amazed at Holmes's clever solutions.

In one story, Holmes dies by going over a waterfall. But Holmes was so popular with readers that Doyle had to bring him back to life and write more stories about him.

See also **mystery.**

People have made homes in many different places, from deserts to rivers. They use many different materials, including animal skins, sod, baked mud bricks (adobe), wood, and glass.

home

A home is a place to live in. It keeps out wind, heat, cold, rain, and snow. Some homes are tents that can be carried from place to place. Homes may also be on wheels. Most people's homes are built on land, but a boat may be a home, too.

Homes differ from place to place. One reason for this is that homes are made to fit the climate. Where the weather is very cold, homes must hold heat well. In warm climates, homes should keep people cool. In temperate climates, a home needs to be warm in winter and cool in summer. Another reason why homes are different is that people use the materials that nature provides. (*See* **building materials.**)

Homes in North America Most settlers in North America built their homes of wood or stone. Parts of the Midwest have very little wood or stone. Settlers there used *sod* —pieces of earth—to build their homes. Eskimo in the Far North used blocks of frozen snow to build *igloos,* homes they used only for a night or two. In parts of the U.S. Southwest, people baked mud bricks called *adobe* to build homes.

Homes Around the World All over the world, people build their homes to suit the environment. In parts of Asia and Africa, houses are built on stilts. These keep the houses above wet ground and protect against floods and wild animals. In moist, tropical areas, wood rots quickly. So people weave tall grasses to build their homes. In the Japanese countryside, where earthquakes are frequent, homes are usually made of lightweight materials. If an earthquake knocks them over, the people inside will not be buried under heavy rubble. *Nomads*—people who travel from place to place—must carry their homes with them. They usually live in tents. (*See* **nomad.**)

Some people have more than one kind of home. Herders change homes with the season, going wherever their animals can find the best food. People who live in city apartments may spend weekends in country cottages or beach houses.

Homes in History The first homes that people lived in were probably caves. Cave dwellers did not spend much time indoors. They used the caves mainly for sleeping, or for protection when the weather was bad.

Little is known about some other early homes. Those made of grass, wood, or mud disappeared thousands of years ago. But sometimes scientists find dirt or rock floors of ancient homes. The pattern of the rooms remains on the floor long after the home itself has disappeared. Scientists have also found piles of animal bones. They know that people made homes from these bones.

Some of the oldest homes still standing are the large castles built for kings and queens. Castles were built of the strongest materials to stand up to enemy attacks. (*See* **castle.**)

Wealthy people had fine homes, too. But even the rich had no central heating, indoor

Apartments have similar spaces, but people make each apartment a home.

plumbing, electricity, or glass windows. Poorer people often had just one or two rooms for a large family. Sometimes, the only pieces of furniture were a table and stools. People spent most of their time working outdoors. They had little time to relax at home.

Homes Today The homes that people live in today would look like palaces to people who lived 200 or 300 years ago. Most have kitchens and bathrooms. Comfortable furniture and electrical appliances make life easier, too.

Some people live in homes built for just one family. Others may live in homes built for two or three families. Many people make their homes in apartment buildings built for hundreds of people.

No matter what kind of home it is, a home is more than just a place to live. For most people, home is the place where they feel most comfortable. It is a welcoming place for family and friends.

See also **architecture.**

Homer

Homer is the name given to an ancient Greek poet. We believe he composed the *Iliad* and the *Odyssey*, two very long poems that tell some of the world's oldest and best-loved stories. The poems are full of adventures that combine legends and real events. Such long poems about heroes are called *epics.*

Very little is known about Homer. Some people are not even sure there was such a person. But most historians say that Homer composed the poems during the 700s B.C.

The *Iliad* takes place during the Trojan War, a war between the Greeks and the city of Troy. The poem begins with events that happened at the end of the war. The Greek hero Achilles and King Agamemnon, leader of the Greek army, have a quarrel. Achilles is so angry that he stays in his tent and refuses to fight. Without him, the Greek soldiers are badly beaten. Achilles' best friend is killed by

Hector, the strongest Trojan soldier. This brings Achilles back onto the battlefield. He is a fierce fighter and kills many Trojans, including Hector. The poem ends with Hector's funeral.

The adventures in the *Odyssey* take place after the Trojan War. It takes the Greek hero Odysseus (who was called Ulysses by the Romans) ten years to return to his home in Greece. Along the way, he and his men stop on an island and are caught by the Cyclops, a one-eyed giant. They escape, only to land on another island, where the goddess Circe turns Odysseus's men into pigs. Circe tells Odysseus that to continue his journey, he must visit the underworld—the place where the souls of the dead dwell. When he returns from the underworld, he must sail through either a whirlwind or rocky waves. She also warns him of the dangerous Sirens, whose

In the *Iliad,* Homer told the story of the Trojan War between Greece and Troy.

singing will lead a sailor to his death. Odysseus is determined to get home. He overcomes all these obstacles.

The *Iliad* and the *Odyssey* began as stories, legends, and history. The stories were

In the *Odyssey,* Odysseus meets many dangers on his trip home from Troy. One is the one-eyed giant Polyphemus, who throws huge rocks at Odysseus's ship.

not written down but were kept alive by being told over and over. Homer combined the stories and composed the verses of the two poems. Homer's long poems were then recited or sung by storytellers. The poems were not written down until later.

See also **Trojan War.**

Homer, Winslow

Winslow Homer was a famous American artist of the 1800s. He is known especially for his paintings of the sea.

Homer was born in Boston in 1836. He taught himself to paint. By the time he was 21, Homer was painting illustrations for magazines. He moved to New York in 1859. *Harper's* magazine sent him to Virginia several times during the Civil War to paint battlefield scenes. Homer also painted scenes showing the lives of black people in the South. He was one of the first artists to do this.

After the war, Homer chose to paint country life—farm people, children, and summer resorts. At first, he used oil paints. Later, he began to use watercolor paints.

Homer visited England in 1881 and spent a year in a fishing village. Here, he first began painting pictures of the sea and of the people who worked on it as fishermen and boatmen. When he brought these paintings back to the United States, they were greatly admired.

In 1883, when he was 47 years old, Homer moved to a lonely spot on the coast of Maine. In Maine, Homer lived quietly and almost never talked to other artists. He went on trips sometimes and did some of his most famous paintings when he traveled.

Homer painted many ocean, mountain, and forest scenes. He showed sailors and others who lived rugged outdoor lives. *Eight Bells* and *The Fog Warning* are two of his most famous paintings of life at sea.

Homer was a *naturalist*—he tried to paint nature as it really is. He used color, light, and design in ways that made his paintings very special. Many paintings by Winslow Homer can be seen in art museums in the United States.

Honduras, *see* Central America

Winslow Homer especially enjoyed painting pictures of boatmen and fishermen at sea. In the painting called *The Herring Net*, fishermen are bringing in their catch.

Hong Kong's harbor has boats of every size, including some that people live on.

Hong Kong

Hong Kong is a British colony on the southeast coast of Asia. It is one of Asia's most important centers of banking, tourism, trade, and manufacturing. Its port, Victoria Harbor, is one of the busiest in the world. Hong Kong became a British colony in 1842. As a colony, it has some self-rule, but a British governor. Great Britain has agreed to return Hong Kong to China in 1997. English and Chinese are the official languages.

Part of Hong Kong lies on mainland China and Kowloon Peninsula. The rest of Hong Kong consists of 236 islands. The capital city, Victoria, is on Hong Kong Island. Victoria Harbor is between Victoria and Kowloon, the major city of Kowloon Peninsula.

Almost all of Hong Kong's 5½ million people are Chinese. About half of the people work in factories producing clothing, toys, watches, and electronic equipment. You may own a digital watch made in Hong Kong. The blue jeans you wear were probably made in Hong Kong.

Hoover, Herbert, *see* presidents of the U.S.

hormone

Hormones are chemicals that control body activities. Some hormones control the balance of salt and water in the cells. Some direct how a child grows into an adult. Others change how fast the heart beats. There are 30 to 40 different hormones.

Hormones are produced by special organs called *endocrine glands.* The endocrine glands release the hormones into the blood. The amount of hormones in the blood must be carefully balanced. Too much or too little of any hormone can cause illness.

For example, the thyroid gland produces a hormone called *thyroxin.* Thyroxin controls how fast the body burns food for energy. If a person's thyroid makes too much thyroxin, the food burns too quickly. The person loses weight and feels very jumpy. But if a person's thyroid makes too little thyroxin, the body burns food too slowly. The person gains weight and feels very tired.

The hypothalamus, a part of the brain, seems to send commands out to the glands by way of the pituitary gland. If another gland is making too little hormone, the hypothalamus sends out signals asking for more. When there is enough of the hormone, the hypothalamus signals the gland to slow down or stop.

See also **gland.**

horse

The horses that people ride and race today are the descendants of ancient wild horses. At first, early people hunted the wild horses for food. Then, about 5,000 years ago, people caught some of the wild horses and tamed them. They trained the horses to pull plows and to let people ride on their backs. People who had horses could farm more land and travel farther.

In many parts of the world, people still use horses for transportation, to pull heavy loads, and to do farm work. In the United States and Europe, people use horses mostly for riding and racing. Some people keep horses as pets.

Features of a Horse The height of a horse is measured from the ground to the shoulders, in units called *hands*. A hand is 10 centimeters (4 inches), the average width of a man's hand. Horses range in height from about 7 hands to 15 hands. The horse's body is covered with a coat of short hair. A mane of long hair runs from the top of the head down along the neck. Long hairs also grow from the tail. The horse uses its tail to swat flies that land on its back and legs.

A horse has long, muscular legs. Its foot is really one big toe. A thick hoof covers and protects the toe. Hooves let the horse run over rough ground without hurting its legs. Horses can run very fast. Running away is a horse's main way of protecting itself against enemies. It will also fight with its hooves and use its teeth to bite.

A horse has four *gaits*—ways of moving—walk, trot, canter, and gallop. The walk is the slowest gait. The trot is faster—like a person jogging. The canter is faster still. The gallop is the fastest gait of all. When a horse gallops, all four feet may be off the ground at

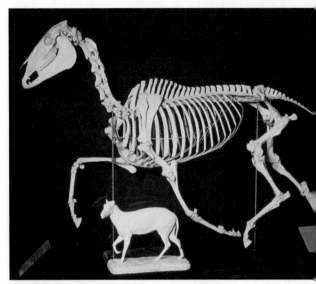

A model of the early horse, eohippus, next to a skeleton of a modern horse. Eohippus was about the size of a dog.

the same time. Some racehorses have galloped short distances at speeds of more than 64 kilometers (40 miles) per hour.

A horse has very good senses of hearing, sight, and smell. Its ears twitch back and forth and pick up the slightest sound. Its big eyes move independently. One eye may be looking at things in front while the other eye is looking at things beside the horse. The nostrils can open wide to take in a lot of air. This helps the horse smell. It also gets large amounts of oxygen into the lungs. The horse needs this oxygen for running.

The only true wild horse is Przewalskii's horse (below), a breed that lives in Asia. At right, a horse's height is measured in *hands* from the ground to its shoulder.

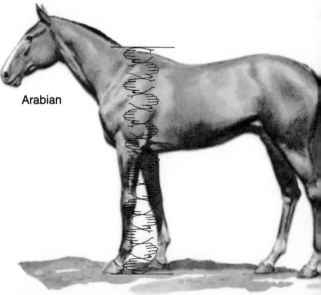

Arabian

Horses are grazing animals—they eat grass and other pasture plants, and they eat a lot. An average horse eats about 12 kilograms (26 pounds) of grass a day. The horse cuts the grass with its 12 sharp front teeth. Then it chews the grass with flat grinding teeth on the sides of its jaws. A horse's teeth never stop growing. But they are worn down by chewing.

Male horses are called *stallions.* Females are *mares.* A newborn horse is called a *foal.* Until they are four years old, male horses are sometimes called *colts,* and female horses may be called *fillies.* A foal is able to stand right after it is born. When it is only a few hours old, it is able to run.

Breeds of Horses There are hundreds of kinds of horses. People have developed different breeds for different uses. The breeds fall into three groups—draft horses, lightweight horses, and ponies.

Draft horses are big and powerful. They may weigh more than a ton. They are used to pull heavy loads. They also are popular circus horses. Clydesdales, shires, and Bretons are draft horse breeds.

Lightweight breeds are slender, streamlined animals. They weigh less than draft horses. They are used for riding and racing. One of the most beautiful lightweight breeds is the Arabian. The Arabian has a small head, small ears, and large dark eyes. It can run very fast and keep running for a long time.

Cowboys like to ride quarter horses because they can quickly stop, start, and turn. Quarter horses and thoroughbreds are popular racing breeds. Another common racing breed is the standardbred. Standardbreds are used for harness racing. In harness racing, the horses do not carry *jockeys*—riders. Instead, each horse pulls a two-wheeled carriage called a *sulky.* A driver in the carriage controls the horse.

The smallest breeds of horses are called ponies. They are sometimes used to carry children and to pull carts. A Shetland pony has a small head, a strong back, and a very full mane and tail. In winter, it has a thick coat.

Wild Horses Przewalskii's horse is the only true wild horse that exists today. It is a small horse with a large head and a short, stiff mane. It lives in central Asia.

The "wild horses" of western North America are not true wild animals. Horses are not native to the Americas. They were brought here by the Spanish in the 1500s. The ancestors of America's "wild horses" are domestic horses that escaped from people or were turned loose. The horses live in herds of one stallion and several mares.

A thoroughbred is a lightweight racing horse related to the Arabian horse.
The Clydesdale is a draft horse. Ponies used to do work, but now are usually pets.

thoroughbred

pony

Clydesdale

hospital

A hospital is a place where sick people can stay while receiving medical tests and treatments to help them get better. A hospital can provide care that a single doctor's office is not equipped to give.

There are different kinds of hospitals. Most illnesses can be treated in a general hospital. Special hospitals care for people of a certain age or with certain illnesses. For example, a pediatric hospital treats only children. Research hospitals conduct medical studies as well as treat patients.

Most general hospitals are divided into units. Each unit is equipped to care for a certain group of patients. For example, the *maternity* unit is for mothers and newborn babies. Children stay in the *pediatric* unit. The *surgical* unit is for patients who need surgery. An *intensive care* unit is for severely ill patients. Some hospitals have a *psychiatric* unit for mentally ill patients. The *emergency* unit is for people who have had bad accidents or are suddenly ill.

An injured boy is treated in the emergency room, where people who have just been injured get immediate attention.

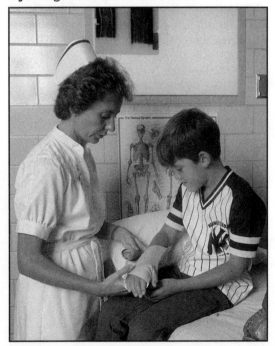

Most hospital treatments require the patient to stay overnight. People who are very sick may stay much longer. Hospitals also provide services for people who do not have to stay overnight. A person may go to a hospital for just a few hours for tests or X-rays.

Hospitals have special machines that help doctors learn what is wrong. X-ray and sonogram machines show what is inside a patient. Other machines show a patient's heartbeat on a television screen, or clean a patient's blood.

Hospitals feed overnight patients healthy meals. Some patients need special diets. The hospital kitchen must prepare many kinds of foods.

A hospital needs to have many people on its staff, doing different jobs. Doctors supervise the treatment of their patients. People who have graduated from medical school must work as *interns* in hospitals before they can become licensed. Then they must work as hospital *residents* in their special fields of medicine. Nurses care for patients according to the doctors' directions. Student nurses also work in hospitals as part of their training.

Besides those who care for patients, many other people work in hospitals. Pharmacists provide the medicines that doctors order for their patients. Dietitians plan healthful menus. Food-service workers make the meals for patients and staff. Laboratory workers test blood, urine, and tissue samples. Therapists help patients overcome physical handicaps. Administrators handle the hospital's business affairs. Many teenagers work in hospitals as volunteers called "candy stripers." The name comes from the stripes on their uniforms.

Early hospitals were usually charity institutions run by churches. The patients were poor city people. Wealthy people preferred treatment in their homes, since hospitals were often dirty and crowded. During the late 1800s, people began to understand that cleanliness helped stop the spread of diseases. Doctors and nurses made an effort to

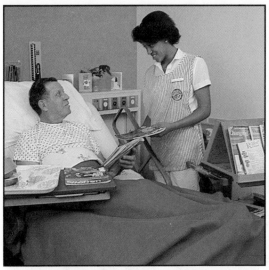

A volunteer "candy striper" brings reading material to patients in this hospital.

keep hospitals clean. People also began to pay for hospital care.

Today, many hospitals work with local governments to be sure that everyone in the community can get good medical care. Hospitals have social workers to help patients with special needs who are leaving the hospital and returning to the community. Hospitals are so important to communities that federal and state governments help pay for some of them.

Before there were hotels and motels, travelers stayed with families or religious groups. A few *inns* also took in travelers. In England in the 1600s, some innkeepers began offering travelers beds, food, and stables for horses. Strangers often had to share rooms.

Some hotels for wealthy people opened in Europe and the United States. In 1829, the Tremont Hotel in Boston offered something new—private rooms with locks on the doors. Later, less expensive hotels opened for traveling business people. In the early 1900s, Ellsworth Statler began building hotels with a bathroom for each room.

When automobile travel became popular, some farmers built *tourist cabins* near the roads. Tourist cabins became a main business for many people. Someone thought of connecting the cabins. They called the places *motels,* from the words *motor* and *hotel.*

House of Representatives, *see* Congress, U.S.

hotels and motels

Hotels and motels are places where travelers can stay. Hotels used to be mainly for people traveling by train or ship. Motels used to be for people traveling by car. Today, there are fewer differences between hotels and motels.

Motels (below) are for people traveling by car. Hotels (right) are mainly for people who arrive by plane or train. They may be downtown or near a vacation attraction.

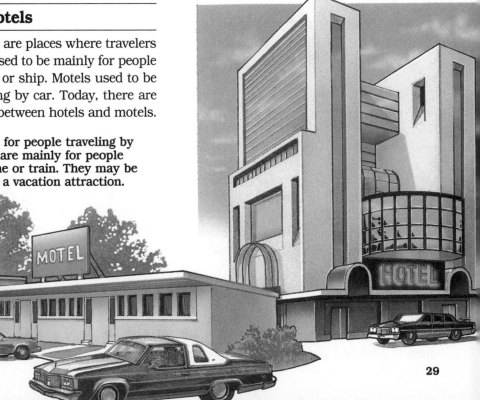

The Johnson Space Center in Houston displays giant rockets that send people into space.

Houston

Houston (HYOUS-ton) in southeastern Texas, is the largest city in the state and one of the largest cities in the United States. Nearly one-quarter of all Texans live in the Houston area. The Houston Ship Canal links the city with the Gulf of Mexico.

Houston was founded in 1836, the year Texas became independent from Mexico. It was named for Sam Houston, who led the Texan army to victory. It became a busy port city after the Houston Ship Canal was built. The discovery of oil in the area brought still more people and businesses.

Today, Houston is the third-busiest port in the United States. It is an important center for oil and natural gas production. It is a manufacturing center, too. Its factories make steel machinery, plastics, and synthetic rubber. Doctors and nurses study at the city's medical centers. The Lyndon B. Johnson Space Center, headquarters for manned space flights, is in Houston. Houston also has the Astrodome, the first sports stadium built with a roof and air conditioning.

Houston, Sam

Sam Houston was the first elected president of the Republic of Texas. He was born in Virginia in 1793, but grew up in Tennessee. At

first, Sam worked in a store, but this was too dull for him. He ran away and lived with the Cherokee Indians for three years.

At age 19, Sam left the Cherokee. He soon joined the army, and was badly wounded in a battle against the Creek Indians. He became a war hero. The people of Tennessee elected him to Congress and later made him governor.

Houston left Tennessee for Texas in 1832. Texans wanted to break away from Mexico and chose Houston to command their army. When Houston's army won the Battle of San Jacinto in 1836, Texas became independent. Grateful Texans elected Houston their president. (*See* **Mexican War.**)

In 1845, Texas became part of the United States. Houston returned to Congress, this time representing Texas. In 1859, he became governor. At the start of the Civil War, Texas wanted to leave the United States and join the Confederacy. Houston was against this, so Texans removed him from office. He died in 1863.

See also **Texas.**

Huang He

The Huang He—Yellow River—is one of the world's great rivers and the second-longest river in China. Only the Chang (Yangtze) River is longer. The Huang He winds east

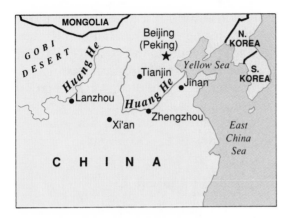

through northern China for about 3,000 miles (4,828 kilometers) before emptying into the Yellow Sea. Ancient Chinese cultures started along the banks of the Huang He. The river valley is fertile farmland.

For the last third of its journey to the sea, the Huang He carries large amounts of fine yellow soil. The soil sometimes chokes the riverbed and the river overflows its banks. In the past, the Chinese built dikes to try to stop the flooding. But the floods continued, and millions of people died. The river earned the name "China's Sorrow."

In recent years, the Chinese have built more dams across the river to control flooding and provide electricity. (*See* **dikes and levees** and **dam**.)

Ships cannot sail the whole length of the Huang He. In some parts, it is too shallow. In others, soil deposits make it run too swiftly.

Hudson, Henry

Henry Hudson was an English explorer who lived in the early 1600s. Very little is known about his life except that he made four voyages. He believed that he could reach Asia by sailing north from Europe around or through North America. This route, called the *Northwest Passage,* would be the shortest way for traders to send goods from Europe to China. (*See* **Northwest Passage**.)

An English company sent Hudson on his first two voyages, in 1607 and 1608. The first time, he sailed along Greenland and into Arctic waters. The second time, he sailed up the west coast of Norway. But each time, he could not find a way through the ice and had to return to England. He did spot many whales in the cold sea, and his reports brought many whale hunters.

A Dutch trading company paid for Hudson's third voyage, in 1609. Hudson sailed his ship, the *Half Moon,* along the east coast of what is now the United States. He explored Chesapeake Bay, and then sailed north to Delaware Bay. In late summer, Hudson entered New York Bay. He sailed up a broad river for some 150 miles (240 kilometers) to where Albany, New York, now stands. This river was later named the Hudson River.

Hudson had failed to find a Northwest Passage. But his voyage gave the Dutch a claim to the land along the Hudson River. Dutch settlers began moving in the 1620s.

On his last voyage, in 1610, Hudson sailed his ship, the *Discovery,* into a large bay, though Hudson thought he had reached the Pacific. This bay later became known as Hudson Bay. (*See* **Hudson Bay**.)

Hudson explored the bay all that summer and fall. But by winter, the *Discovery* was locked in ice. Hudson and his men had to wait for spring.

By spring, Hudson's men were sick, starving, and angry. One day, they rebelled. Hudson, his son, and seven other men were

On his third voyage, Hudson discovered the Hudson River. On a fourth voyage, he discovered Hudson Bay.

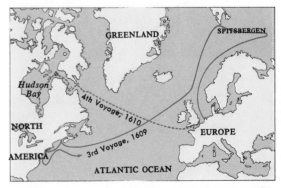

forced into a small boat and set adrift. They were never seen again. When Hudson's ship returned to England without him, the men were thrown into prison.

Hudson's last voyage had important results. The English were able to claim all the land in Canada around Hudson Bay. They began a fur trade there that was to bring them wealth for many years.

Hudson Bay

Hudson Bay, in northeast Canada, is one of the largest inland seas in the world. It is about half the size of the Mediterranean Sea. Millions of people live near the Mediterranean, but very few people live near Hudson Bay. The land there is very cold, and the bay is frozen over for most of the year.

Hudson Bay is bordered by the Canadian provinces of Manitoba, Ontario, and Quebec, and by Canada's Northwest Territories. The bay is connected to the North Atlantic Ocean by Hudson Strait. Dozens of small rivers run into Hudson Bay.

Some Eskimo live along the northern shores of the bay. Indians live along the western and southern shores, especially around James Bay, a fingerlike extension of Hudson Bay.

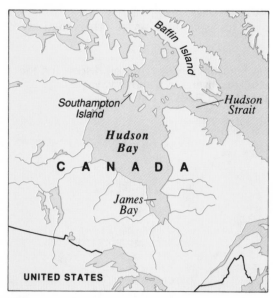

Hudson Bay was discovered in 1610 by the English explorer Henry Hudson. He was looking for a route to the Pacific Ocean. (*See* **Hudson, Henry** and **Northwest Passage.**)

Churchill is the most important port on Hudson Bay. But ships can travel to and from Churchill only between July and October, when the bay is not frozen.

Hughes, Langston

James Langston Hughes, a great black American writer, was born in Missouri in 1902. As a young man, he worked at odd jobs. He worked on a boat and as a hotel busboy. *Weary Blues,* his first book of poems, was published in 1926, when Hughes was only 24 years old. He graduated from college in 1929.

Langston Hughes wrote poetry about the thoughts and feelings of black people in the United States.

Hughes was a member of what is called the "Harlem Renaissance" in New York in the 1920s. This was a sort of awakening among black artists, writers, and musicians. For the first time, many black Americans were writing of their experiences. Hughes was a leader among the poets.

Hughes put jazz rhythms into his poems. In fact, many of his poems were later set to music. He wrote stories, too, which can be read in a collection called *Ways of the White Folk*. He also wrote plays and novels, and two autobiographies, *The Big Sea* and *I Wonder as I Wander*.

Langston Hughes died in New York City in 1967. People called him the "Poet Laureate of Harlem." Though this is not an official title, it shows how highly people thought of Langston Hughes. A poet laureate is usually a nation's most respected poet.

human body

Nothing humans have invented is as amazing as the human body. We continue to discover how the parts of the body work together and balance each other.

We sometimes compare our bodies to machines. The hands are like pliers that pick things up and put them down. The heart is a pump that pushes blood through blood vessels like tiny pipes. The brain is like a huge computer, but can do many more things. The nerves are like the telephone wires in a large city, carrying messages to and from different places in the body. The stomach and intestines are like power plants. They change fuel into energy for our bodies.

Yet our bodies are very different from machines. Machines do not grow, and cannot repair themselves when they are broken. They do not laugh or cry, or live in families, or know how to help each other. Machines also cannot reproduce themselves.

Comparing the body to human inventions can help us understand how it works. The brain is like a powerful computer, and the eye is like a camera. The heart and the lungs are pumps—one for liquid and one for air. The skeleton is like a framework of pipes, and a hand can grasp things like pliers do.

Muscles (on the left of the figure) help to hold the body skeleton together and to move it. Underneath the muscle layer is the bony skeleton (on the right of the figure). In addition, there are internal organs, such as the stomach and intestines. Not shown are the networks of nerves and blood vessels.

Systems of the Human Body The human body has many different organs and parts. They work together in complicated ways. One way to see how our body parts and organs work together is to think of them as different *systems.*

Skin doesn't seem like a system, but it is a very important one. It protects the inside of the body from the outside world. It keeps dirt and germs from getting inside and making us sick. Skin also keeps the body's heat and moisture inside. If the skin is hurt by a cut or a scrape, other body systems go to work to repair it. Together with two other systems—the skeleton and the muscle system—skin helps give the body its shape. (*See* **skin.**)

The **skeleton** is made of the bones inside the body. It is the frame that holds the body up. Without a skeleton, you would not be able to sit up, or even move. Bones in the skeleton also protect other parts of the body. For example, the skull covers the brain, and ribs protect the lungs and heart. (*See* **skeleton** and **bone.**)

The **muscle** system makes the body move. One kind of muscle is made of stretchy material. One end is attached to one bone and the other end is attached to another bone. When the muscle bunches up, it moves one of the

Amazing facts about the human body

1. More than half your body is made of water!

2. If you put all your blood vessels in a straight line, they would stretch 100,000 miles!

3. You have more than 200 bones! More than 100 of them are in your hands and feet.

4. You have more than 600 muscles!

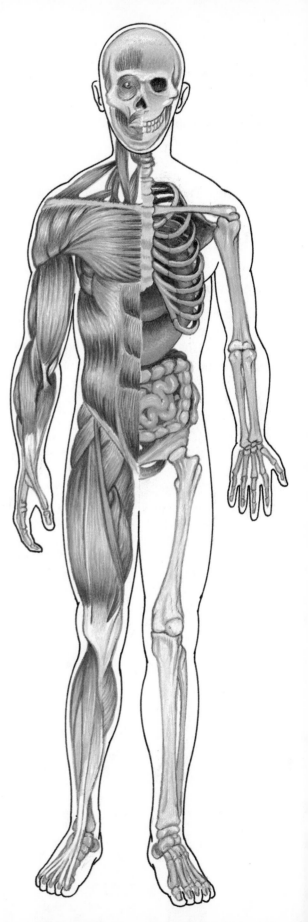

bones. For example, when you bunch up the muscle along the top of your upper arm, your arm bends at the elbow.

Other muscles help move food through the stomach and intestines. One very special muscle causes the heart to pump. The heart pumps more than 100,000 times every day! (*See* **muscle** and **heart.**)

The other systems carry out activities that are needed to keep us alive. The **digestive system** changes food into a form our bodies can use for energy. It sends this special fuel into the blood so that it can be carried to all parts of the body. The digestive system also moves waste materials out of the body. (*See* **digestion.**)

The **respiratory system** helps us breathe. Breathing is the way we get oxygen from the air. Our bodies need oxygen as well as fuel to make energy. The nose, the windpipe, and the lungs are parts of the respiratory system. (*See* **breathing.**)

The **circulatory system** moves blood through the blood vessels. The blood vessels form a network that is over 60,000 miles (96,000 kilometers) long. Blood carries oxygen and fuel to all parts of the body. It carries waste products to the kidneys and to the lungs, where the wastes are removed. Blood also contains white blood cells, which help protect the body from disease. (*See* **blood circulation.**)

The **immune system** protects us from viruses and from the bacteria that cause disease. Even when we do not feel sick, our bodies have small infections that the immune system is stopping. The antibodies and the white blood cells that do the work of the immune system flow through blood vessels and the **lymph system.** The lymph system is another network of vessels. We sometimes say we have "swollen glands" when the sides of our necks swell and hurt. These swollen glands are the lymph system at work, fighting an infection. The lymph system also collects fluids that have leaked from the blood vessels and returns them to the blood vessels. (*See* **antibody.**)

The **urinary system** removes waste materials from the blood. The main parts of the urinary system are the kidneys, two organs just below the ribs in the back. As blood passes through the kidneys, the kidneys take out waste products called *urine.* The urine is stored in a sac called the *bladder* until it leaves the body. (*See* **kidney.**)

The **reproductive system** enables people to have children. The male reproductive system produces sperm cells. The female reproductive system produces egg cells. If a sperm and egg cell unite inside a woman's body, a new human being begins to grow and develop. After nine months in the mother's uterus, the baby is ready to be born. (*See* **reproduction** and **birth.**)

The **endocrine system** is made up of many glands. Glands make the chemicals, called *hormones,* that help control the way other body systems work. Hormones are important to growth, digestion, reproduction, and many other body functions. (*See* **gland** and **hormone.**)

The brain, spinal cord, and sense organs are parts of the **nervous system.** The brain allows us to think and remember. It can also send messages to the muscles telling them how to move. The senses include hearing, seeing, smelling, tasting, and feeling. The spinal cord is the link between the brain and the rest of the nervous system. The nervous system directs the activities of all the other body systems. It keeps all the different parts of the body working together smoothly. (*See* **brain** and **nerve.**)

Cells All the different parts of the body are made of tiny building blocks called *cells.* Different kinds of cells do different jobs. A muscle cell can stretch and tighten. A nerve cell carries messages from one part of the body to another. A skin cell is flat, like a piece of cloth.

Most cells are so small that they cannot be seen without a microscope. Your body has billions of cells. Each cell contains a "blueprint" for your entire body. (*See* **cell** and **genetics.**)

humidity

Water evaporates from oceans, lakes, and rivers. It changes from a liquid to a gas, called *water vapor,* and goes into the air. Humidity is the amount of water vapor in the air.

The amount of water vapor that air can hold depends on the air's temperature. Warm air can hold more water vapor than cold air. Air is at its *dew point* when it contains as much moisture as possible at that temperature. If the temperature drops below the dew point, some of the water vapor changes into ice—frost—or back into water —dew. (*See* **dew** and **frost.**)

Relative humidity is the amount of water vapor in the air compared to the total amount the air can hold. If the air holds half as much water vapor as possible, the relative humidity is 50 percent. When the air is at its dew point, the relative humidity is 100 percent. Knowing the relative humidity helps us predict rain or frost. (*See* **weather** and **weather forecast.**)

You cannot see water vapor, but you can feel its effect. On hot days with high humidity, your sweat cannot evaporate easily. Your skin feels sticky. On days with low humidity, your sweat dries quickly.

hummingbird

Hummingbirds are small, brightly colored birds. The largest is less than 23 centimeters (9 inches) long and weighs 23 grams (3/4 ounce). The smallest bird of all is the Cuban bee hummingbird. It is only 5 centimeters (2 inches) long—about as big as your pinkie—and weighs only 2 grams (1/14 ounce).

Hummingbirds are the only birds that can fly backward. They can hover in one place or quickly dart away. Hummingbirds beat their wings so quickly that the wings blur and make a humming sound. Most hummingbirds beat their wings 50 to 70 times per second. The violet hummingbird may beat its wings up to 80 times per second!

This hummingbird hovers in the air while taking nectar from a flower.

All this activity uses up a lot of energy. Like all animals, hummingbirds get energy from the food they eat. But they must eat a lot of food for their size. They eat almost all day long. They drink nectar from flowers and eat spiders and insects.

All hummingbirds have long beaks. The sword-billed hummingbird has a beak as long as its head and body! The tongue of a hummingbird is long, too. It is used as a tube to suck up nectar and other liquids from inside flowers.

Hummingbirds are aggressive birds. They fight among themselves and attack enemies by diving at them. Hummingbirds will attack birds much bigger than themselves. They even will attack people who disturb them.

During courtship, the females watch while the male hummingbirds perform dances in the sky. After the birds mate, the female builds a nest shaped like a tiny bowl. She glues it to a tree with spider's webs. Some hummingbirds build nests that hang like a cradle from a branch, a leaf, or the eaves of a roof. In her nest, the female lays two white eggs about the size of peas. When the young hummingbirds hatch from the eggs, they are blind and without feathers. The mother bird takes care of her young until they can fly.

Hummingbirds live only in the Americas. Most kinds live in the tropics, but some live in the desert and on high mountains. The ruby-throated hummingbird is common in eastern North America. The rufous hummingbird lives in western North America. These birds migrate. In autumn, they fly south to warmer places. In spring, they return to their northern homes. Hummingbirds that live in the tropics stay in the same area all year. (*See* **migration.**)

See also **bird.**

Hungary

Capital: Budapest
Area: 35,919 square miles (93,030 square kilometers)
Population (1985): about 10,644,000
Official language: Magyar (Hungarian)

Hungary is a small country in Eastern Europe. It is landlocked—surrounded by other countries and without a seacoast. Bordering Hungary to the north is Czechoslovakia. The Soviet Union lies to the northeast. Romania is to the east, Yugoslavia is to the south, and Austria is to the west.

In 1867, Hungary joined Austria to form the Austro-Hungarian Empire. This empire ruled much of central Europe until the end of World War I. Hungary then became an independent country. In the late 1940s, Hungarian Communists took control of the country. In 1956, the Hungarians revolted against communist rule. But the revolt was stopped with help from the Soviet Union. Over 200,000 Hungarians fled their country.

Hungary's farms produce corn, wheat, and potatoes. Bauxite, an ore that contains aluminum, comes from Hungary's mines.

Franz Liszt and Béla Bartók are Hungary's two most famous composers of music.

Towns on two sides of the Danube River, Buda (left) and Pest (right), joined to form Budapest, Hungary's capital city.

37

hunting

For thousands of years, people hunted wild animals for food. They used the fur, feathers, and skins to make clothing and rugs.

Before early people learned to farm, they moved from place to place in search of food. They gathered plants to eat and hunted animals. They learned ways to make hunting easier. By hunting in a group, they could kill a very large animal, or chase birds and other small animals into a net. People set traps and made spears, knives, and arrows to help them catch and kill animals.

Most hunting today is done for sport. In the United States, deer and ducks are two of the most popular kinds of *game*—animals hunted for sport. Deer hunting is done by *stalking*—the hunter follows the animal until it is close enough to shoot. Duck hunting requires the hunter to stay in one place and wait for a duck to swim or fly by. This is called *still hunting.*

Until recently, there were few laws to control hunting. Certain kinds of animals were in danger of extinction because hunters killed so many of them. Today, laws forbid hunting certain animals. Other animals may

A duck hunter sets out *decoys*—wooden ducks—to get wild ducks to land nearby.

be hunted only in certain seasons. This helps to keep animal populations from growing too small or too large.

Huron, Lake, *see* Great Lakes

hurricane

Hurricanes are large, whirling windstorms that form over tropical areas in the western Atlantic Ocean. These storms have violent winds and drenching rains. They cause huge waves and high tides. Heat and moist air keep the storms going.

Similar storms occur in other seas. In the western Pacific Ocean, they are called *typhoons.* In the Indian Ocean, they are called *cyclones.* Storms near Australia are called *willy-willies.*

What Makes a Hurricane Hurricanes start over vast areas of calm water near the equator. These regions are far from shore, where no breezes from land disturb the air.

Almost all hurricanes occur in summer and fall. During summer, the calm ocean water steadily grows warmer. The air above it becomes warmer, too. It fills with the water vapor that evaporates from the ocean. This large area of warm, moist air rises high above the sea. Cooler air rushes in from all sides to replace it. The onrushing air starts to spin. The warm, moist air is pushed inward and upward in a spiral.

High in the air, the warm, moist air spreads out and cools. The water vapor changes back into water. As the winds blow harder, spinning clouds form around a calm, clear area called the *eye.* Driving rains pelt down. The air rises faster and faster, creating violent winds. The winds rage around the hurricane's eye at 110 to 240 kilometers (74 to 150 miles) per hour. The air pressure in the eye falls rapidly. The winds whip the sea into huge waves.

A full-size hurricane is 480 to 960 kilometers (300 to 600 miles) across. From a weather satellite, the eye looks something

A hurricane creates damaging winds and tides along the Gulf of Mexico and the Atlantic. A satellite view (above left) shows a powerful hurricane that is 300 miles across.

like a doughnut hole. Around the hole are the strongest winds and heaviest rain. But within the eye, all is calm and clear. The eye is usually about 15 to 30 kilometers (10 to 20 miles) across. Some people are fooled by the calm, clear sky of the hurricane's eye. They think the storm has passed, so they leave their shelter. But they are battered by the storm as soon as the eye passes.

When a hurricane moves over land or over colder ocean waters, it loses its energy source. It cannot get enough moisture or heat. Obstacles on the land slow down the hurricane. Gradually, the storm dies. The average hurricane lasts about six days.

Killer Hurricanes Hurricanes that start in the Caribbean usually move west and then north or northeast. Some die at sea, but many reach land. The southeastern coast of the United States is most often hit by these hurricanes. Some areas farther north have also been badly damaged.

In September 1900, a killer hurricane roared across the Caribbean and into the Gulf of Mexico. Galveston, Texas, located on an island, was hit full force. The wind-driven seas created a *storm surge.* Waves higher than 4.5 meters (15 feet) swept over the island. Most of the city's buildings were destroyed. At least 6,000 people were drowned. (*See* **flood.**)

In 1938, a destructive hurricane swept north along the eastern coast of the United States. The hurricane whipped across Long Island and slammed into Connecticut. It moved so fast that it was later called the "Long Island Express." A storm surge with huge waves washed over the shores of Connecticut, Rhode Island, and Massachusetts. The waves and high winds smashed boats and broke up piers. On land, powerful winds uprooted trees and knocked down small buildings. Heavy rains soaked New England. Rivers overflowed and caused flooding. By the end of the storm, about 600 people had lost their lives. About $300 million worth of property damage had been done.

Hurricanes and Meteorologists The U.S. National Weather Service names all the hurricanes that form in the Caribbean Sea. The first hurricane of a year is given a name that begins with *A.* The next one is given a name that begins with *B,* and so on. Boys' and girls' names are used alternately.

Weather forecasters can usually predict when a tropical storm will develop into a hurricane. They can tell which way the storm is moving, and warn people or ships in the area. But a hurricane cannot be stopped. By being prepared, people can prevent some of the damage and reduce loss of lives. (*See* **weather forecast.**)

hybrid seed

Many farmers plant their crops using hybrid seeds. A hybrid comes from fertilizing a plant with pollen from another plant of a slightly different type. The resulting hybrid seed develops into a plant that is a cross between the two parent plants. Hybrid seeds usually produce healthier plants.

Much of what is known about hybrid seeds was discovered from breeding corn plants. In corn, the tassel is the male part of the plant. Grains of pollen are produced in the tassel and carried by wind to the silk of the corn plant. The silk is the female part of the plant. Silk that has been pollinated produces the kernels of corn, which are really seeds. It is easy to produce hybrid seed from corn. If you have two kinds of corn in a field, you can remove the tassels from one kind. Then all the corn will be pollinated by the other kind.

By the 1950s, well over 90 percent of all corn plants came from hybrid seeds. Today, hybrid seeds are used to produce many fruits and vegetables—from big, flavorful strawberries to juicy, vitamin-rich tomatoes.

See also **farming; heredity; genetics;** and **plant breeding.**

hydrogen

Hydrogen is the most common element in the universe. It makes up 75 percent of all matter. It is also the lightest element. As a gas, hydrogen is tasteless, odorless, and colorless. It is the main part of water. Its name comes from two Greek words that mean "water giver."

Hydrogen makes the sun and stars burn brightly. In the center of the sun and the stars, hydrogen atoms are changed into helium, the second-lightest element. This change, called *fusion,* releases tremendous amounts of energy—heat, light, and radiation. Most of the sun's energy goes into space. A small amount reaches the earth and makes life possible.

On the earth, hydrogen occurs in combination with other elements. In water, it is combined with oxygen. In plants, animals, and fossil fuels, it is combined with carbon.

To get hydrogen gas from water, the hydrogen must be separated from the oxygen. A strong electric current is sent through the water. This makes the hydrogen leave the oxygen, and it is then collected as hydrogen gas.

Because hydrogen is the lightest element, the gas was once used to fill balloons. But at the slightest spark, hydrogen gas combines explosively with the oxygen in air. Today, helium is used instead. It is not as light as hydrogen, but it will not explode.

The main industrial use for hydrogen gas is in the production of ammonia. Ammonia is made by combining hydrogen and nitrogen. Ammonia is used mostly to make fertilizers to help plants and crops grow.

Liquid hydrogen and oxygen are used as fuels to launch spaceships and satellites into space. We also combine hydrogen and oxygen to develop hot flames that can weld and bond metal plates.

Hydrogen is everywhere—in the sun and in water. It is also used as a rocket fuel.

These young plants grow without soil. They are "planted" on a plastic sheet. The roots get all their nutrients from the water underneath.

hydroponic gardening

Hydroponic gardening is a way of growing plants without soil. Instead, plants grow in fertilized water, or in coarse gravel covered with water. People have experimented with growing plants in water since 1697.

Most hydroponic gardening is done in greenhouses. Young plants grow in long, shallow containers filled with water. Mixed into the water are plant nutrients. Plants require 17 nutrients. Among them are nitrogen, potassium, iron, calcium, phosphorus, and magnesium. (*See* **greenhouse.**)

Hydroponic plants can be grown indoors in any season. They grow faster than they would in a field. They are also cleaner. But greenhouses are expensive to build and to maintain, so hydroponic gardening costs more than outdoor gardening.

Today, hydroponic gardening is done in many parts of the United States. It is used in the northeastern part of the country to meet the high demand for fresh vegetables in winter. Some of the most popular hydroponic crops are leaf lettuce, salad spinach, herbs, tomatoes, and cucumbers.

hyena

Hyenas look like large dogs. But they are not related to dogs. One of the major differences between them is the legs. A dogs four legs are all about the same length. But a hyena's front legs are longer than its back legs. This gives the hyena a sloping back and a clumsy walk.

Hyenas are carnivores—meat-eaters. They sometimes hunt live animals, but usually they *scavenge*—look for dead animals to eat. They watch lions or a pack of wild dogs make a kill. After the lions or dogs have finished eating and left the animal's carcass—its dead body—the hyenas move in. They eat whatever is left. Their strong jaws and teeth can even crack and eat bones.

There are three kinds of hyenas. The largest and best-known is the laughing hyena. It is also called the spotted hyena because its

The spotted hyena is a scavenger—it eats meat left by other animals, such as lions.

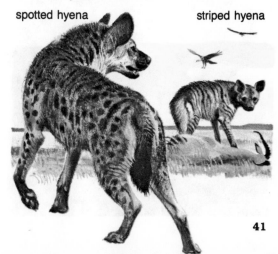

spotted hyena   striped hyena

fur is marked with many dark spots. This hyena may weigh as much as 80 kilograms (175 pounds). It lives in Africa south of the Sahara Desert. The sounds it makes are some of the strangest made by any animal. One cry sounds like a laugh. Another cry starts as a low, deep growl and rises to a very high sound. Laughing hyenas usually run in packs.

The two other kinds of hyenas do not live in packs. The striped hyena lives in Asia and North Africa. The brown hyena lives in South Africa.

hypnotism

The act of hypnotism places a person in a condition that is somewhere between sleep and complete wakefulness. Unlike a sleeping person, a person who is hypnotized can walk and talk. But the person usually moves and talks in response to suggestions given by the *hypnotist*—the person who does the *hypnotizing.*

The hypnotist first tries to relax the person who wants to be hypnotized. The hypnotist may do this by repeating the sentence "You are very tired." The hypnotist will also

A hypnotized woman and the hypnotist. Hypnosis can be used to help break bad habits such as smoking or overeating.

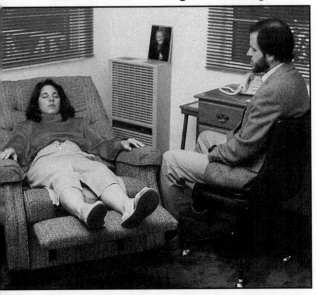

tell the person to stare at something small—a pencil point, a candle flame, or a swinging watch.

While hypnotized, a person is open to the hypnotist's suggestions. For example, if a hypnotized person is told that he or she will feel no pain, the person will not feel pinpricks or pinches. At the hypnotist's request, a shy child might sing for an audience. A hypnotized person may remember events he or she could not remember when awake.

Hypnotism can be done safely by someone who is properly trained. But the careless use of hypnotism by untrained people can be very dangerous to the hypnotized person.

hypothesis

A hypothesis is a prediction—a guess—about what will be discovered by an experiment. Not just any guess will do as a hypothesis. It has to be based on what the scientist already knows and has observed.

You make hypotheses, too. Suppose a friend buys a new sweater and asks you to guess its color. If you guess just any color, you are making a wild guess. But you might remember that your friend's favorite color is blue. If you say "Your new sweater is blue," your guess is based on information. This is a hypothesis.

A scientist tests a hypothesis by doing an experiment. You may make the hypothesis that cats purr when they are stroked. You can test it by stroking several cats. If they all purr, you know that your hypothesis is correct. If some purr and some do not, you know that your hypothesis is sometimes correct. If none of the cats purr, you know that your hypothesis is never correct.

Scientists use information they get from testing one hypothesis to come up with new hypotheses. Even when a hypothesis is proved incorrect, scientists learn something. They find out that they should try other ideas, and the experiment may give them information they did not have before.

See also **experiment.**

The letter I began with the Egyptian word picture for "hand." It was also used by the Semites.

The Phoenicians changed the way it was written. They called it *yod*, their word for "hand."

The ancient Greeks were the first to write the letter by making a single stroke.

ice age

Imagine New York City, Cleveland, Chicago, and Seattle covered year-round with ice hundreds of yards thick. About 11,000 years ago, the regions where these cities stand today actually were completely covered with ice. The earth was having one of its ice ages. Ice ages are times during the earth's history when temperatures are so low that ice covers large areas of the planet.

Recent Ice Ages Throughout most of its existence—about 4½ billion years—Earth has been warm. The average temperature at the surface has been about 21° C (70° F). But every 150 million years or so, the earth has gone through a period of cooling. Such a period lasts 1 or 2 million years. During that time, temperatures drop by about 7° C (13° F)

During the last ice age, ice covered more than half of North America and Europe.

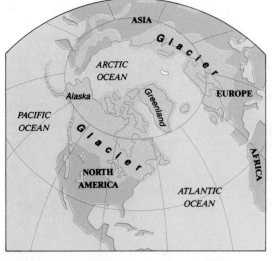

on average. Whenever this happens, bodies of permanent ice, called *ice sheets* and *glaciers,* begin to grow. They spread out until they cover as much as a third of the earth's land area. (*See* **glacier.**)

Geologists have found evidence of four ice ages in the earth's history. The oldest one happened about 600 million years ago. There was another ice age 450 million years ago, and a third one 300 million years ago. The most recent ice age began about 2 million years ago. Some geologists think this ice age ended about 10,000 years ago, when the great ice sheets retreated from Europe and the northern United States. But others say that it is not over yet. They believe that the earth is now in a temporary warm period called an *interglacial.* After the interglacial passes, the ice will slowly start to spread out again.

Evidence of Ice Ages What evidence do geologists have that the ice ages ever happened? They know that glaciers and ice sheets cause a kind of erosion called *glaciation.* Geologists study areas where glaciation is happening now. These include Greenland, Alaska, Antarctica, and the high peaks of mountain ranges. They see that erosion by glaciers and ice sheets produces certain kinds of deposits. When they find such deposits in an area, they know that long ago the area was covered by ice.

One kind of deposit produced by glaciation is called *till.* Till is a jumble of clay, sand, gravel, rocks, and boulders. It is unlike any other kind of deposit produced by erosion. The till produced during the ice ages is

43

found in many places. Till from earlier ice ages has turned to rock. Till from the most recent ice age is easier to recognize. In North America, the recent ice sheet extended to a line that crossed the northern United States. Deposits of till are found north of this line in New England, New York, New Jersey, Pennsylvania, and Ohio.

In many areas, deposits of till from the last ice age are familiar landmarks. In some places, they form a long, low ridge called a *terminal moraine.* A terminal moraine runs down the center of Long Island, New York, a distance of over 161 kilometers (100 miles).

When the amount of ice increases, the amount of water in the oceans decreases. One result of an ice age is that sea level drops all around the world, exposing more land. During the last ice age, sea level was 90 meters (300 feet) lower than it is now. When the ice melted, valleys were drowned by the sea. Chesapeake Bay, on the eastern shore of the United States, was once such a valley. Norway's fiords were valleys once, too. (*See* **fiord**.)

Fishermen trawling off the coast of North America have brought up the bones of *mastodons* and *mammoths*. These extinct relatives of the elephant lived during the last ice age. They roamed areas of the continental shelf—the ledge of land extending out underwater from the continent—that are now under hundreds of feet of ocean water.

Causes of Ice Ages Scientists have various ideas about why ice ages come and go, and why warm periods—interglacials—come between periods of cold. Some scientists think ice ages are caused by the motion of our solar system. They say that as our solar system travels through its galaxy, the Milky Way, it sometimes enters areas of space dust. The space dust can be so thick that it reduces the amount of sunshine that reaches the earth.

During an ice age, the changing periods of cold and warmth may be caused by changes in the earth's orbit. These changes happen over the course of about 90,000 years. The tilt of the earth changes over a period of 40,000 years. This, too, may cause periods of cold and warmth.

See also **climate** and **earth history**.

iceberg

In the cold, polar regions of the world, glaciers and ice sheets reach into the sea. Where the ice meets the sea, huge blocks break off. These blocks are icebergs. Icebergs float, because ice is lighter than liquid water.

This region on the shore of Hudson's Bay in Canada was once covered by giant glaciers. The rocks were smoothed and polished by the huge sheets of ice.

Icebergs seem huge on top of the water (above), but may be ten times larger under the water (right).

Some float thousands of miles, crossing the routes used by oceangoing ships. In 1912, the ocean liner *Titanic* sank after it ran into a drifting iceberg.

The ice from glaciers and ice sheets is made of fresh water. Sailors in need of water to drink have sometimes been able to get it from icebergs.

Most icebergs break off from the glaciers and ice sheets of Greenland and Antarctica. The largest icebergs are the ones that come from Antarctica. One of the largest ever seen was a little over 320 kilometers (200 miles) long and 97 kilometers (60 miles) wide.

Icebergs float low in the water. We can see only a small fraction—about one-ninth—of an iceberg. The rest is underwater. A tall iceberg, one that rises 61 meters (200 feet) or more above the surface, may reach down more than 305 meters (1,000 feet) below the waves.

As an iceberg drifts into warmer seas, it gradually melts and breaks apart.

See also **glacier.**

ice cream

Ice cream is a sweet frozen dessert. It is made from cream and milk, water, sweeteners, and flavorings. Other items may be added, such as fruit and nuts.

Like milk, ice cream has vitamins and minerals. But ice cream has more fat and sugar than milk does. Many doctors say ice cream is good for people who do not have to lose weight.

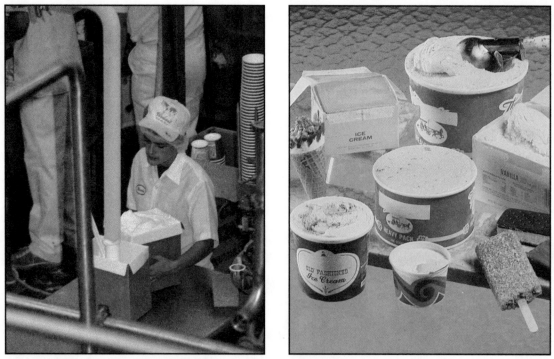

An ice-cream factory may produce thousands of gallons of ice cream a day. The ice cream is packed into containers, shaped into bars, or put in cones.

Nobody knows who made the first ice cream. People in ancient Rome enjoyed ices flavored with fruit juices. Marco Polo returned to Italy from China with stories about a frozen dessert. The first ice cream was probably made in Italy. In the 1700s, ice cream came to America.

At first, ice cream was made at home in special freezers. These freezers had an outer compartment and an inner compartment. The outer part was packed with ice and salt to keep the inside cold. The ingredients were placed in the inside compartment. The freezer had a crank that was turned by hand. This mixed the ingredients and added air, which made the mixture smoother. Some people still make ice cream at home in old-fashioned freezers or in one of the newer electric machines.

In 1851, Jacob Fussell of Baltimore, Maryland, opened the first ice-cream factory in the United States. By the early 1900s, ice-cream parlors opened. They served plain ice cream, sundaes, ice-cream sodas, and other treats.

Ice cream made in a factory goes through several steps. First, the milk products are mixed with sugar and water. Then this mixture is *pasteurized*—heated enough to kill any germs. After that, it is *homogenized* —thoroughly mixed—to make it smoother. It goes first into a cooler and then into a storage tank. Afterward, flavorings are added. Then it goes into a freezer. Finally, it is packed into containers. In 1984, in the United States alone, 884 million gallons of ice cream were manufactured.

Several desserts are similar to ice cream. Ice milk is not as rich as ice cream, because it is made with milk instead of cream. Sherbet is usually made with egg whites and fruit juices. Tofu, which is made from soybeans, is used for making a frozen dessert without any milk products.

Today, ice cream comes in hundreds of flavors. Vanilla is the favorite, followed by chocolate and strawberry.

ice hockey, *see* hockey

Iceland

Capital: Reykjavik
Area: 39,768 square miles (102,999 square kilometers)
Population (1985): about 241,000
Official language: Icelandic

Iceland, "the land of fire and ice," is an island country in the North Atlantic Ocean. Its northern tip just touches the Arctic Circle. Huge ice sheets called *glaciers* cover part of the land. But Iceland also has hundreds of hot springs, geysers, and volcanoes. Icelanders use the hot springs' heat to warm their homes. Many of the volcanoes are still active, and lava covers parts of the island.

Most Icelanders live along the southern coast, where the ocean keeps the climate mild. Over half live in Reykjavik, the capital and largest city. Reykjavik is a modern city with a university and an orchestra. It is also Iceland's largest port.

Some of the world's richest fishing waters are around Iceland. Many people make their living either by fishing or by working in factories that process fish.

Iceland was discovered by the Irish around the year 800. Soon after, it was settled by Vikings from Norway. Norway ruled the island for about 500 years. Then it was ruled by Denmark. In 1944, Iceland became an independent country.

ice-skating, *see* skating

This giant ice cave in Iceland has hot-water springs inside.

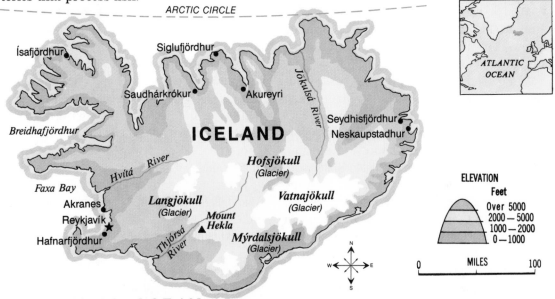

ARCTIC CIRCLE

Ísafjördhur

Siglufjördhur

ATLANTIC OCEAN

Saudhárkrókur • Akureyri

Jökulsá River

Seydhisfjördhur

Breidhafjördhur

ICELAND

Neskaupstadhur

Hvítá River

Hofsjökull (Glacier)

Faxa Bay

Akranes

Reykjavik

Hafnarfjördhur

Langjökull (Glacier)

Mount Hekla

Thjórsá River

Vatnajökull (Glacier)

Mýrdalsjökull (Glacier)

ELEVATION
Feet
Over 5000
2000 – 5000
1000 – 2000
0 – 1000

N
W   E
S

0   MILES   100

ATLANTIC OCEAN

47

Idaho

Capital: Boise
Area: 83,564 square miles (216,431 square kilometers) (13th-largest state)
Population (1980): 943,935 (1985): about 1,005,000 (40th-largest state)
Became a state: July 3, 1890 (43rd state)

Idaho is a state in the northwestern United States. When Idaho is mentioned, many people think of large Idaho baking potatoes, one of the state's most important products.

Land Even though it is known for its farmland, most of Idaho is mountainous. On a map, it has a wide, flat southern part and a long, narrow part, called the *panhandle,* reaching north to Canada.

The panhandle is in the Rocky Mountains and is covered by thick forests, including the largest stand of white pine trees in the world. In the central part of the state, the mountains are even higher and more rugged. The highest point is Borah Peak. It is 12,662 feet (3,859 meters) high.

Most of southern Idaho is part of the Columbia Plateau, a region of high, rolling plains. The plateau has rich soil, but it must be irrigated for farming.

Idaho's largest river is the Snake River. It begins in the Rocky Mountains in eastern Idaho and winds across the Columbia Plateau. Then it turns north and becomes part of the border between Idaho and Oregon. Along this part of the river is Hells Canyon, the deepest gorge in North America. In some places, the gorge is 7,900 feet (2,408 meters) deep—more than a mile and a half from rim to bottom. Hells Canyon is more than 100 miles (161 kilometers) long.

Majestic bighorn sheep, elk, bear, and mountain lions thrive in Idaho's mountain wilderness. Strange "kissing" frogs live in rushing streams. The frogs' mouths can grab onto a rock like suction cups, to keep them safe in rapids.

Idaho is known for its natural wonders. Craters of the Moon in southeastern Idaho, a national monument, is an eerie place. Thousands of years ago, hot melted rock and cinders escaped from deep inside the earth. They formed a fantastic landscape where few plants can survive. Idaho also has many ice caves—underground caverns coated with ice.

People Not many people live in Idaho, compared with other states. Large areas of Idaho have fewer than two people per square mile. Most of the people live on the farmlands irrigated by the Snake River.

The capital and largest city is Boise. About 100,000 people live in Boise. It is a transportation, trade, and supply center for gold mines and farms in the area around it.

The state's early settlers came from the East and the Midwest. The Mormons moved to Idaho from Utah in search of farmland, and still form Idaho's largest religious group. There is also a large colony of Basques, people from Spain who first came to work as shepherds. The Basques brought with them many of their folk festivals and customs.

History Nez Percé, Shoshone, and other Indian tribes have lived in Idaho for at least 4,000 years. The first white men to visit the area were the explorers Meriwether Lewis and William Clark, who came to Idaho in 1805. (*See* **Lewis and Clark Expedition.**)

After them came fur traders and missionaries. When gold was discovered in Idaho in 1860, the first permanent settlers arrived. As they took over the Indians' land, fierce wars broke out. Now the few Indians who are left live on reservations.

For many years, the territory that contains Idaho was claimed by both the United States and Great Britain. It became part of the United States in 1846. The Idaho Territory was formed in 1863. It also included land in what are now Montana and Wyoming. Boise was named its capital.

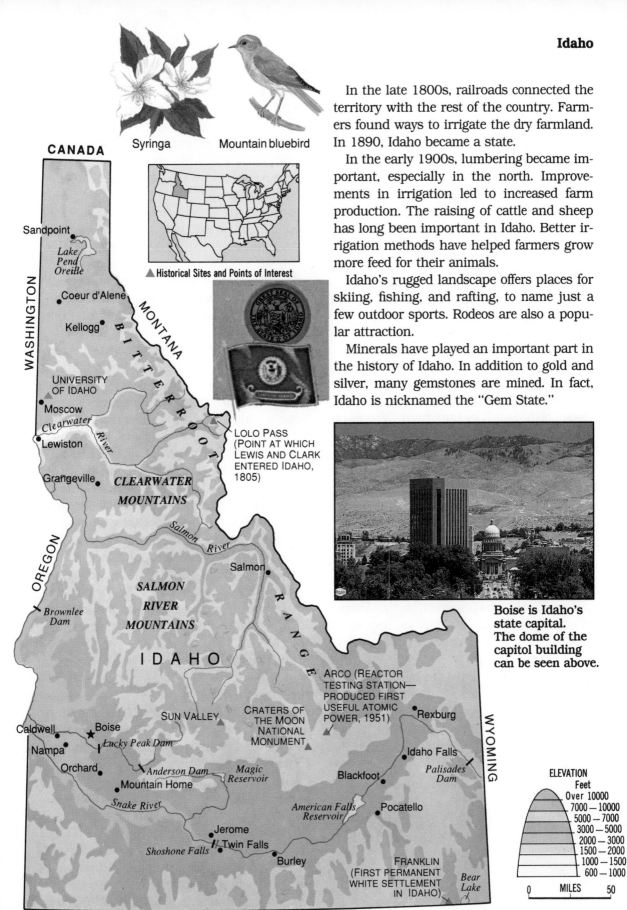

Syringa   Mountain bluebird

CANADA

▲ Historical Sites and Points of Interest

WASHINGTON

Sandpoint

Lake Pend Oreille

Coeur d'Alene

Kellogg

MONTANA

BITTERROOT

UNIVERSITY OF IDAHO

Moscow

Clearwater River

Lewiston

Grangeville

CLEARWATER MOUNTAINS

LOLO PASS (POINT AT WHICH LEWIS AND CLARK ENTERED IDAHO, 1805)

Salmon River

Salmon

OREGON

SALMON RIVER MOUNTAINS

Brownlee Dam

RANGE

I D A H O

ARCO (REACTOR TESTING STATION— PRODUCED FIRST USEFUL ATOMIC POWER, 1951)

Rexburg

Caldwell   Boise

SUN VALLEY

CRATERS OF THE MOON NATIONAL MONUMENT

Lucky Peak Dam

Nampa

Orchard

Anderson Dam

Magic Reservoir

Idaho Falls

Palisades Dam

Blackfoot

Mountain Home

Snake River

American Falls Reservoir

Pocatello

Jerome

Shoshone Falls   Twin Falls

Burley

FRANKLIN (FIRST PERMANENT WHITE SETTLEMENT IN IDAHO)

Bear Lake

WYOMING

ELEVATION
Feet
Over 10000
7000 – 10000
5000 – 7000
3000 – 5000
2000 – 3000
1500 – 2000
1000 – 1500
600 – 1000

0   MILES   50

NEVADA   UTAH

In the late 1800s, railroads connected the territory with the rest of the country. Farmers found ways to irrigate the dry farmland. In 1890, Idaho became a state.

In the early 1900s, lumbering became important, especially in the north. Improvements in irrigation led to increased farm production. The raising of cattle and sheep has long been important in Idaho. Better irrigation methods have helped farmers grow more feed for their animals.

Idaho's rugged landscape offers places for skiing, fishing, and rafting, to name just a few outdoor sports. Rodeos are also a popular attraction.

Minerals have played an important part in the history of Idaho. In addition to gold and silver, many gemstones are mined. In fact, Idaho is nicknamed the "Gem State."

Boise is Idaho's state capital. The dome of the capitol building can be seen above.

Illinois

Capital: Springfield
Area: 56,400 square miles (146,076 square kilometers) (24th-largest state)
Population (1980): 11,427,409 (1985): about 11,535,000 (5th-largest state)
Became a state: December 3, 1818 (21st state)

The state of Illinois is in the Midwest, the heartland of the United States. On a map, Illinois looks something like an Indian arrowhead pointing south. It is connected to its neighboring states by important waterways, railways, and highways.

Illinois is more than 800 miles from the Atlantic Ocean. But there are two ways to travel all the way from Illinois to the Atlantic by ship! You can sail north from Chicago through the Great Lakes and the St. Lawrence River to the Atlantic. Or you can travel south on the Mississippi River to the Gulf of Mexico, which connects with the Atlantic.

Illinois has good farmland and large reserves of coal. Good transportation and natural resources make Illinois an important state for manufacturing and trade.

Land Much of the area that is now Illinois was scraped nearly flat by the glaciers that covered it millions of years ago. Glaciers also made the soil rich and fertile. The state has hot summers and cold winters. The hot summers and high rainfall—nearly 40 inches (100 centimeters) a year—are very good for farming. (*See* **glacier**.)

Illinois leads the nation in growing soybeans and is second only to Iowa in growing corn. Much of the corn is used to feed hogs and cattle.

People Nearly two-thirds of the people of Illinois live in or near Chicago. Chicago is the state's largest city and the second-largest in the nation. It is a major center for iron and steel production, meat-packing, and grain trading. It is also a major railroad center. The area has many important museums and universities. (*See* **Chicago**.)

The rest of the people live in smaller towns and cities throughout the state. Springfield, the state capital, is in central Illinois. Abraham Lincoln lived there before he became president of the United States. The state is sometimes called the "Land of Lincoln."

People of many different racial and ethnic backgrounds live in Illinois. Some are descendants of people who immigrated from Europe in the late 1800s and early 1900s. Large groups of immigrants came from Germany, Ireland, Scandinavia, Poland, Italy, and Greece. Many of these people have kept their European customs. Chicago also has a large population of black Americans.

History Prehistoric Indians known as the Mound Builders lived in what is now Illinois. Later, Illinois Indians—a confederacy of related tribes—controlled the area. Starting in the middle 1600s, Iroquois Indians moved in. They eventually drove out the Illinois.

French explorers, missionaries, and fur traders were the first Europeans to visit Illinois. They set up trading posts and missions in the late 1600s. Then in 1763, Britain defeated France in the French and Indian War. Britain won France's North American lands—including the Illinois region. (*See* **French and Indian War**.)

In 1800, the Illinois region became part of the Indiana Territory, which was the western portion of the Northwest Territory. Nine years later, it split from Indiana and became the Illinois Territory. In 1818, Illinois became a state.

The early settlers of Illinois wanted land that belonged to the Indians. In 1832, the United States went to war against Chief Black Hawk and his tribes. The Indians were defeated and left Illinois. Soon, many more farmers moved there. Better plows and reaper machines were invented. This meant farmers could work the hard ground, plant

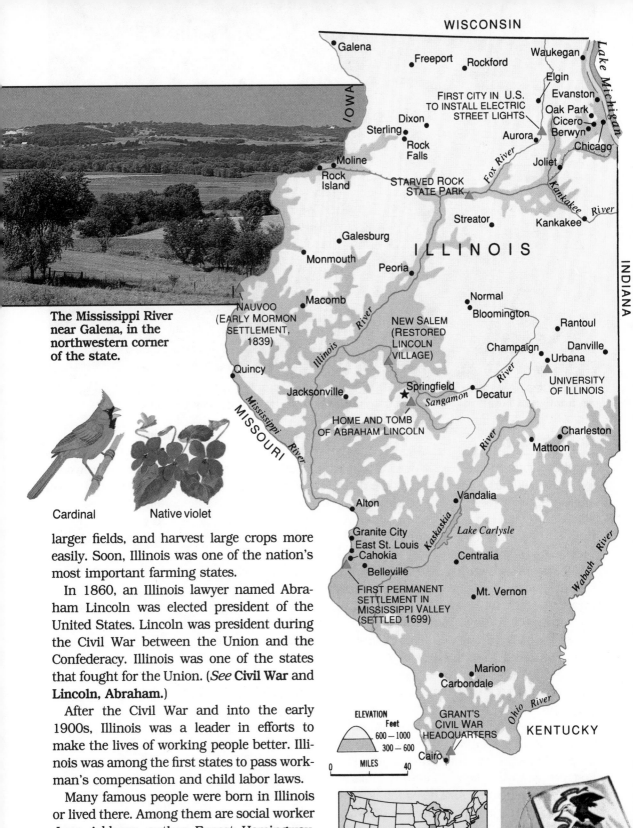

WISCONSIN

IOWA

• Galena

• Freeport • Rockford

• Waukegan

Lake Michigan

• Elgin

FIRST CITY IN U.S.
TO INSTALL ELECTRIC
STREET LIGHTS

• Evanston
Oak Park •
Cicero •
Berwyn •

• Dixon

• Sterling
Rock •
Falls

Aurora •

Fox River

• Chicago

• Moline

Rock •
Island

STARVED ROCK
STATE PARK

Joliet •

Kankakee River

• Streator

Kankakee •

INDIANA

• Galesburg

I L L I N O I S

• Monmouth

Peoria •

• Normal

Illinois River

NEW SALEM
(RESTORED
LINCOLN
VILLAGE)

Bloomington •

• Rantoul

• Macomb

NAUVOO
(EARLY MORMON
SETTLEMENT,
1839)

Champaign •

• Danville
Urbana •

UNIVERSITY
OF ILLINOIS

• Quincy

★ Springfield •
Decatur •

Sangamon

Jacksonville •

HOME AND TOMB
OF ABRAHAM LINCOLN

River

• Charleston

Mattoon •

MISSOURI

Mississippi River

• Vandalia

Lake Carlysle

Wabash River

• Alton

Kaskaskia

• Granite City
East St. Louis •
• Cahokia

• Centralia

• Belleville

FIRST PERMANENT
SETTLEMENT IN
MISSISSIPPI VALLEY
(SETTLED 1699)

• Mt. Vernon

ELEVATION
Feet
600 — 1000
300 — 600

• Marion

• Carbondale

GRANT'S
CIVIL WAR
HEADQUARTERS

Ohio River

KENTUCKY

0   MILES   40

Cairo •

The Mississippi River
near Galena, in the
northwestern corner
of the state.

Cardinal   Native violet

larger fields, and harvest large crops more
easily. Soon, Illinois was one of the nation's
most important farming states.

In 1860, an Illinois lawyer named Abraham Lincoln was elected president of the
United States. Lincoln was president during
the Civil War between the Union and the
Confederacy. Illinois was one of the states
that fought for the Union. (*See* **Civil War** and
Lincoln, Abraham.)

After the Civil War and into the early
1900s, Illinois was a leader in efforts to
make the lives of working people better. Illinois was among the first states to pass work-
man's compensation and child labor laws.

Many famous people were born in Illinois
or lived there. Among them are social worker
Jane Addams, author Ernest Hemingway,
poet Carl Sandburg, President Ronald Reagan and architect Frank Lloyd Wright. (*See*
**Addams, Jane; Reagan, Ronald; Wright,
Frank Lloyd;** and **American writers.**)

▲ Historical Sites and Points of Interest

An immigrant family arrives in the United States from Italy in the early 1900s.

immigration

Immigration is the process by which people leave their homes in one land and settle in another. When people leave the country where they were born, they are *emigrating* from it. When they enter their new country, they are *immigrating* to it.

The words *emigrating* and *immigrating* both contain the word *migrating,* which means "wandering from one place to another." Human beings have been migrating across the earth throughout their history. At first, they lived as hunters and gatherers. They went where there were herds of animals or plenty of wild plants. Sometimes, they were driven away from their homes by natural disasters, such as floods or droughts.

North and South America were populated by people migrating from other lands. The first people to live here, American Indians, probably came from Asia to what is now Alaska. They gradually moved southward and eastward to both continents. Another great migration was the movement of Europeans to the Americas. Between 1650 and 1950, close to 70 million people left Europe to come to the Americas.

Reasons for Immigration Why did so many people choose to leave their homelands? Europe was growing very crowded. Farmers could not find land to farm. People in the crowded cities often could not find jobs. The Americas offered vast stretches of open land to farmers. Growing industries offered jobs. These economic opportunities acted as a magnet to many people seeking an escape from poverty.

Another magnet was the promise of greater freedom. Sometimes, people in Europe were not allowed to practice their own religion. Some were also forced to support a religion in which they did not believe. They emigrated so that they could have religious freedom.

Others emigrated in search of political freedom. Some wanted to escape wars that were raging in their countries. Others came to escape governments that treated them harshly.

From the early 1600s until the early 1800s, a very large group came to the Americas from Africa. They did not come by choice. They were the millions of black Africans who were brought here to work as slaves on plantations and in mines.

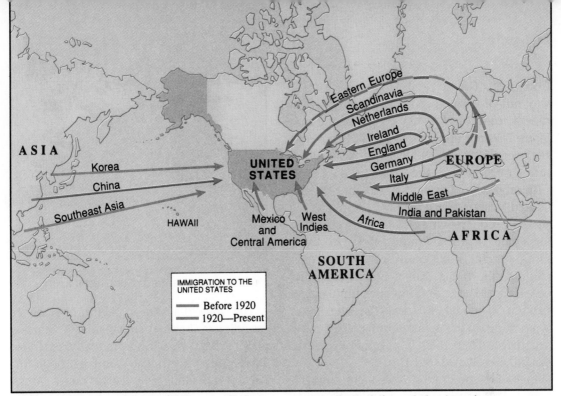

Early immigrants came from Europe. Today, more come from Asia and the Americas.

A Nation of Immigrants The United States has often been called a "nation of immigrants." It has taken in more immigrants than any nation in history. In fact, except for pure-blooded American Indians, every U.S. citizen is either an immigrant or descended from immigrants.

The first European immigrants to what is now the United States began arriving in the early 1600s. They came mainly from Great Britain. Many of them—like the Pilgrims and Puritans in New England and the Catholics in Maryland—came to find religious freedom. They were soon joined by settlers from the Netherlands and Sweden. In the late 1600s, thousands of Germans, also seeking religious freedom, settled in Pennsylvania.

By the time the country declared its independence in 1776, there were about 2 million people of European descent living in it. There were also about half a million black Africans. In the next 40 years, immigrants continued to come from Europe, a few thousand each year.

Then, beginning in the 1820s, immigration became a flood. Times were hard in Germany. So, by the 1840s, as many as 60,000 German immigrants were arriving in the United States each year. At the same time, the potato crop in Ireland failed for several years in a row. Over a million Irish immigrants fled to the United States.

In the late 1840s, Chinese immigrants began arriving on the Pacific coast. They helped to build the railroads linking the West Coast and the East Coast.

At first, most European immigrants came from countries in northern and western Europe. Beginning in 1885, more immigrants began coming from countries in southern and eastern Europe. Some were poor people

These immigrants from Vietnam run a store in Portland, Oregon.

from Italy, Greece, and Poland, seeking a way out of their poverty. Some were Jews, mostly from Russia. They came seeking religious freedom and an escape from poverty. Between 1890 and 1930, nearly 25 million immigrants entered the United States.

Immigration Laws Not everyone in the United States favored so much immigration. In 1882, Congress passed a law forbidding any more Chinese immigration. In 1929, Congress said that no people from Asia could settle in the United States. This law also limited the total number of immigrants to 150,000 a year. In the 1940s, the limits were raised to allow immigration of Europeans driven from their homelands by World War II. (*See* **World War II.**)

In 1965, immigration laws were changed again. The ban on Asian immigration was removed and the limit for all immigrants was raised to 290,000 people per year.

Today, many immigrants to the United States come from Asia and from Latin America. These include Mexicans and people from Central and South America and the Caribbean islands. Most come desperately seeking work, because they cannot find jobs in their own countries.

Unfortunately, more people want to come than the limit allows. Therefore, many enter the country without the U.S. government's permission. They are called *illegal aliens.* Every year the number of illegal aliens living in the United States grows.

See also **citizenship.**

immunity, *see* disease and sickness; antibody; vaccine

Inca

The Inca were American Indians who ruled a large empire in South America in the 1400s. They were conquered by the Spanish in the 1530s. Descendants of the Inca live in Peru in the Andes Mountains and still speak Quechua, the Inca language.

Women in a village in Peru grind corn as their Inca ancestors did centuries ago.

The Inca date their beginnings to the founding of Cuzco, their capital city. Starting about 1200, the Inca gradually extended their power north and south through the Andes and along the Pacific coast. At its greatest, their empire stretched over 2,500 miles (4,000 kilometers) from north to south. It covered parts of what are now Colombia, Ecuador, Peru, Bolivia, Argentina, and Chile. Conquered peoples had to learn the Inca language and worship Inti, the Inca sun-god. They also had to pay a tax in the form of crops.

The Inca were fine builders. In Cuzco and other cities, they built huge walls, temples, and palaces. The stones are held together with interlocking joints, not with mortar. The Inca fitted huge stones together so tightly that it is impossible to slide a knife blade between them.

The most amazing building project of the Inca was their road system. Altogether, there were more than 10,000 miles (16,000 kilometers) of roads. Gifts and taxes were brought to the rulers in Cuzco over the roads. But the roads were used mainly for moving soldiers and supplies.

Government messengers traveled along the roads, too. A messenger carried a *quipu* —a cord with knotted strings hanging from it. The arrangement of the knots helped the messenger remember the message. Messengers ran in relays. Each one ran his part of the route as swiftly as possible and then passed the quipu on to the next messenger.

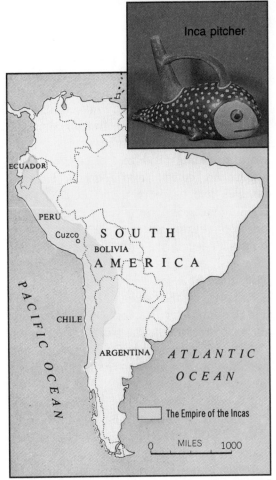

Inca pitcher

A message could be carried 700 miles (1,125 kilometers) in three days. No other people could send messages so quickly until the invention of the telegraph in the 1800s.

Inca farmers grew corn, potatoes, and a grain called quinoa. They raised guinea pigs for meat. Llamas were used as pack animals. The Inca wove the wool from llamas, alpacas, and vicuña into cloth.

In 1532, a small group of Spaniards led by Francisco Pizarro invaded the Inca empire. They tricked and caught Atahuallpa, the Inca ruler. They agreed to set him free if they received two roomfuls of silver and one of gold. The Spaniards got some of the gold and silver, but killed Atahuallpa anyway. The Spaniards marched to Cuzco, and in a few months, the Inca empire fell.

See also **Pizarro, Francisco.**

Independence Day, *see* **Fourth of July**

Independence Hall

Independence Hall is often called the "birthplace of the United States." This stately building was built in the 1730s. It served as the Pennsylvania State House.

In 1775, representatives of the 13 colonies came to Independence Hall to discuss the colonies' problems. This group of men, called the Second Continental Congress, decided that the colonies must break free of Britain. They approved the Declaration of Independence on July 4, 1776. A few days later, the Declaration was read aloud in the State House yard and celebrated with the ringing of the State House bell. This bell was later renamed the Liberty Bell. (*See* **Liberty Bell.**)

Fourteen years later, representatives of the 13 states again met in the State House. This time, they wrote the Constitution, the supreme law of the United States.

Independence Hall is now part of Philadelphia's Independence National Historical Park. The inkstand used by the representatives when they signed the Declaration of Independence is still on display. So is the chair that George Washington used while he directed the Constitutional Convention.

See also **Revolutionary War; Declaration of Independence;** and **Constitution of the United States.**

Thousands of Americans visit Independence Hall in Philadelphia each year.

India

Capital: New Delhi
Area: 1,266,595 square miles (3,280,481 square kilometers)
Population (1985): 767,681,000
Official language: Hindi

India is a country in southern Asia. It is slightly smaller than the United States, but has three times as many people. In fact, India has more people than any country in the world except China. It is one of the most crowded nations on earth.

Land India's southern half is a large peninsula surrounded on three sides by parts of the Indian Ocean. The part to the east is called the Bay of Bengal. The part to the west is the Arabian Sea. The northern half of India borders the countries of Pakistan, Afghanistan, China, Nepal, Burma, Bhutan, and Bangladesh.

India is a land of great extremes. Along its northern borders are the Himalaya Mountains, the tallest in the world. The Thar Desert in the northwest is one of the driest places on earth. Dense rain forests in central India are among the wettest places on earth. India is home to some of the world's great wild animals, including tigers and elephants. Yet it also has rich farmlands and huge cities.

India's farmlands grow huge amounts of food to feed its population. The most productive farmlands are in the Northern Plains, at the foot of the Himalayas. Many rivers run through this region. The most important is the Ganges. Rice is the most important crop.

Farther south is the hilly Deccan region. Growing crops is difficult here. Much of the land is used for grazing animals.

In most of India there are two seasons—a rainy season and a dry season. The rains begin in June and last until September. Damp winds called *monsoons* sweep in from the Indian Ocean, bringing the heavy rains with them. During the dry season—October through May—there is very little rain.

People Most people in India make their living from farming. India is one of the world's leading producers of rice, bananas, sugarcane, cotton, and tobacco. Farming families live in more than 500,000 small farming villages. Most of these village people have no running water or electricity in their homes. They farm with simple tools and grow only enough food to feed their families. They have little left over to sell.

Millions of other Indians live in large cities. Bombay, Calcutta, and Delhi are among the largest cities in the world. Seven other Indian cities have more than 1 million people. City dwellers work in trading businesses and in factories.

Two of the world's great religions started in India. The Hindu religion began in India about 3,500 years ago. Buddhism started about 2,500 years ago.

Today, about four out of five people in India follow the Hindu religion. Many Hindus believe in a *caste* system. They believe that every person is born into one of five castes. People in low castes cannot live in the same neighborhood with people in high castes, or send their children to the same schools. The government of India is working to end the caste system so that all people will be treated more equally. (*See* **Hinduism.**)

Islam is the second-largest religion in India. Its followers are called Muslims. There are also Christians, and followers of other, smaller religions.

History Some of the world's earliest civilizations began in India. The Indus Valley civilization grew along the Indus River in northwest India more than 4,000 years ago. This ancient people built cities with brick houses and orderly streets.

Around A.D. 700, Muslim conquerors from the west invaded northern India. They converted many of the people of present-day Pakistan, India, and Bangladesh to Islam.

In the 1400s, explorers and traders from Europe began making trips to India. They wanted to trade with Indian princes for spices, jewels, and beautiful rugs and fabrics. Traders from France, Holland, and Portugal set up trading posts in India. But the most powerful Europeans were the British. They formed the British East India Company to ship spices and other goods back to Britain. In 1858, the British government made India a British colony.

In the 1940s, many Indians united to fight for independence. They were led by Mahatma Gandhi. Without armies and guns, he was able to force Britain to grant India its independence. (*See* **Gandhi, Mahatma.**)

Today, India is a very important country. It trades with many countries and has many scientists and other professionals. But it is

A busy street in Benares, one of India's many large cities.

still a poor country, with millions of people who have barely enough to eat. People in India are working hard to make life better for all the country's people.

57

Indiana

Capital: Indianapolis
Area: 36,185 square miles (93,719 square kilometers) (38th-largest state)
Population (1980): 5,490,212 (1985): about 5,499,000 (14th-largest state)
Became a state: December 11, 1816 (19th state)

Indiana is a small state in the midwestern United States. It calls itself the "Crossroads of America." Important waterways, railways, and highways have crossed the state since the 1830s. Indiana touches Lake Michigan in the northwest, and part of its southern border is the Ohio River.

Land Millions of years ago, northern Indiana was covered by glaciers—huge sheets of ice. When the glaciers melted, they left flat plains with fertile soils. Summers in Indiana are warm, and winters are cold. The state gets plenty of rain and snow. The rich soil and good rainfall have made Indiana a leading farm state. Corn is the major crop. It is used mainly to feed Indiana's most valuable livestock—hogs.

In northwestern Indiana, wind has carried sand in from Lake Michigan to form large dunes. In some places, the wind has blown the sand away again, uncovering forests that were buried thousands of years ago! There are many vacation homes among the dunes.

The hills of southern Indiana contain huge deposits of limestone and sandstone. People use the limestone for buildings. Indiana produces more building stone than any other state. Limestone is also used in processing iron ore and in making Portland cement.

Underground streams have carved great caves in the soft limestone. Wyandotte Cave in southern Indiana is one of the largest caves in the world.

History The first people to live in Indiana were Mound Builders—prehistoric Indians who buried their dead in mounds. During the 1700s and 1800s, many Indian tribes lived in Indiana.

French explorers and fur traders were the first Europeans in the area. They set up forts along rivers in the early 1700s. French settlers built villages near the forts for protection against the British and the Indians.

In 1763, Britain defeated France in the French and Indian War. The British took over French lands in North America, including Indiana. Many settlers moved to Indiana from the British colonies in the east. (*See* **French and Indian War.**)

When the colonies became the United States, Indiana became part of the Northwest Territory. In 1800, the western portion of the Northwest Territory became the Indiana Territory. Settlers fought with the Indians there. In 1811, the Indians were defeated at the Battle of Tippecanoe. Five years later, Indiana became a state.

Indiana was important in the early history of the automobile. The first car with a clutch and an ignition system was made in the city of Kokomo in 1894. Many factories for producing car parts were built in Indiana. The Indianapolis Motor Speedway became the most famous auto racetrack in the world.

The region around the city of Gary became a great industrial center in the early 1900s. Steel mills there used iron that came from Minnesota by ship through the Great Lakes. They also used coal from nearby Illinois, and limestone from Indiana.

People Most people in Indiana live in or near the cities. Almost all of Indiana's people were born in the United States. The rest have come mainly from Germany. The northern cities have many black Americans. Gary was one of the first U.S. cities to elect a black mayor.

Indianapolis, the capital and largest city, is located in the middle of the state. It is an important manufacturing and transportation center. Each year, 500,000 people crowd the

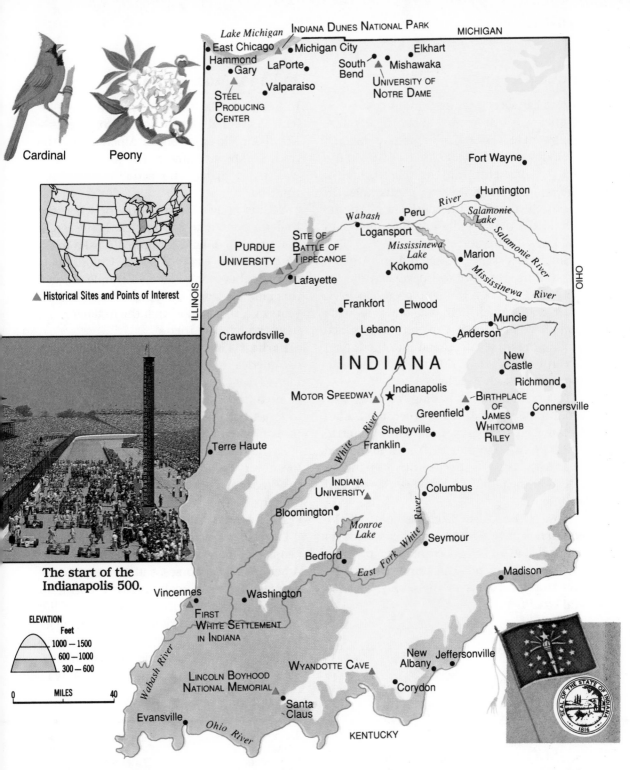

Cardinal

Peony

▲ Historical Sites and Points of Interest

ELEVATION
Feet
1000 – 1500
600 – 1000
300 – 600

0   MILES   40

The start of the
Indianapolis 500.

Lake Michigan
INDIANA DUNES NATIONAL PARK
MICHIGAN
East Chicago
Hammond
Gary
LaPorte
Valparaiso
Michigan City
South Bend
Elkhart
Mishawaka
UNIVERSITY OF NOTRE DAME
STEEL PRODUCING CENTER

Fort Wayne
Huntington
Salamonie Lake
Salamonie River
Wabash River
Peru
Logansport
Mississinewa Lake
Marion
Mississinewa River
Kokomo
OHIO

PURDUE UNIVERSITY
SITE OF BATTLE OF TIPPECANOE
Lafayette

Frankfort
Elwood
Lebanon
Muncie
Anderson

Crawfordsville

INDIANA

New Castle
Richmond

MOTOR SPEEDWAY
★ Indianapolis
BIRTHPLACE OF JAMES WHITCOMB RILEY
Connersville

Greenfield

Shelbyville
Franklin

White River

Terre Haute

INDIANA UNIVERSITY

Columbus

Bloomington

Monroe Lake

Seymour

East Fork White River

Bedford

Madison

Vincennes
Washington

New Albany
Jeffersonville

FIRST WHITE SETTLEMENT IN INDIANA

WYANDOTTE CAVE

Corydon

Wabash River

LINCOLN BOYHOOD NATIONAL MEMORIAL
Santa Claus

Evansville
Ohio River

KENTUCKY

SEAL OF THE STATE OF INDIANA 1816

ILLINOIS

Indianapolis Motor Speedway to watch the "Indianapolis 500"—a 500-mile (805-kilometer) auto race. (*See* **auto racing**.)

Most of the people in southern Indiana live in small villages in the hills. Some of these "uplanders" raise animals or are artists or craftspeople. A few of the villages in the area have surprising names—such as Pumpkin Center, Santa Claus, and Gnaw Bone.

Indiana's nickname is the "Hoosier State." No one is sure where the name came from. It may have come from an old English word, "hoozer," meaning "hill dweller," or maybe from the old pioneer greeting "Who's here?"

Indian Ocean

The Indian Ocean is the third-largest ocean in the world. It covers about 28,356,300 square miles (73,442,480 square kilometers). It stretches more than 6,000 miles (9,677 kilometers), from the eastern shore of Africa to the western shore of Australia. On the south, it washes the continent of Antarctica. In the north, India juts into the ocean and gives it its name.

Since early times, Arab, Indian, African, and Chinese sailors have navigated the Indian Ocean. They brought goods to each other and spread their religions. Vasco da Gama, a Portuguese explorer, first sailed around the tip of Africa and into the Indian Ocean in 1497. He had found a way for Europeans to reach Asia by sea.

Today, instead of sailing all the way around the tip of Africa to reach the Indian Ocean, ships can sail from the Mediterranean Sea through the Suez Canal to the Red Sea. The Red Sea opens into the Indian Ocean at the Gulf of Aden. (*See* **Suez Canal** and **Red Sea.**)

Most of the Indian Ocean is south of the equator, and the ocean water is warm. As winds blow over the ocean, they pick up moisture. The winds can bring heavy rains and tropical storms to the ocean's islands and coasts.

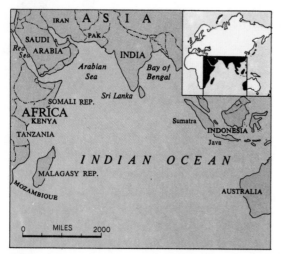

Indians, American

Indians were the first people to live in America. They had settled both continents—North America and South America—by the time Europeans came to the New World. It was the Indians who actually discovered America.

No one knows for sure how or when the Indians first came to America. Long ago, a narrow strip of land connected Alaska to Siberia, in the eastern Soviet Union. It is thought that small bands of people crossed this land bridge. It disappeared over 14,000 years ago, so we know that the Indians must have come before then.

Earliest Times When the Indians came to America, they had a very simple way of life. They hunted wild animals with stone-tipped spears. In fact, the first people to cross the land bridge from Siberia were probably hunters.

As the years passed, Indians moved into almost every region of America. They invented new tools and weapons, including the bow and arrow. They learned how to grow crops, such as corn, beans, and potatoes.

Life was harder for the Indians than for people in many other parts of the world. America had no horses, cattle, sheep, goats, or pigs. These animals are very useful to man. Without them, the Indians' way of life could not advance very far. Still, in what is now Mexico and South America, Indians made roads, built cities, and worked out systems of writing. (*See* **Aztec; Inca;** and **Maya.**)

SOME INDIAN TRIBES

Desert Peoples (Southwest)	**Wigwams and Canoes (Eastern Woodlands)**
Apache	Cherokee
Navajo	Chippewa
Pueblo	Choctaw
	Delaware
	Huron
	Iroquois
	Massachuset
	Potawatomi
	Shawnee

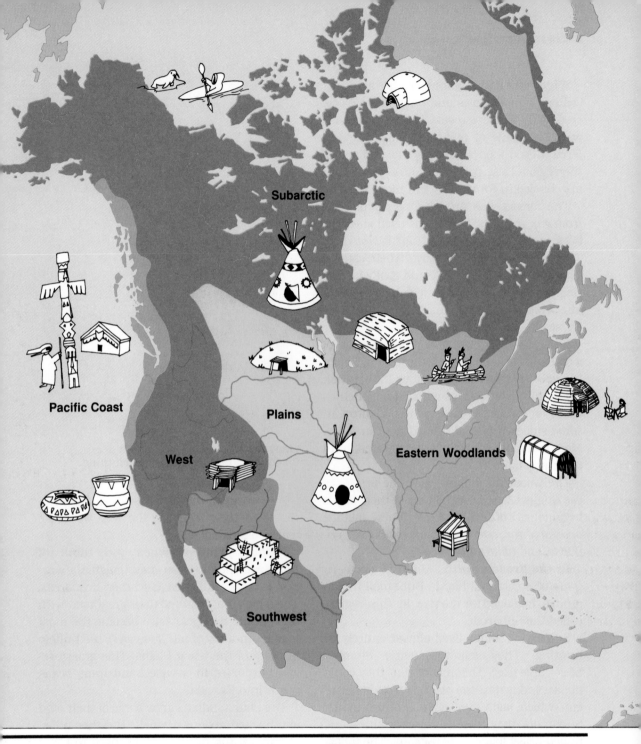

Subarctic

Pacific Coast

Plains

West

Eastern Woodlands

Southwest

In the Frozen North (Subarctic)	Buffalo Hunters (Plains)	Digging and Gathering (West)	Totem Pole Indians (Pacific Coast)
Chipewyan	Arapaho	Flathead	Chinook
Cree	Blackfoot	Maidu	Haida
Hare	Cheyenne	Nez Percé	Kwakiutl
Kutchin	Comanche	Paiute	
Tanaina	Crow	Pomo	
	Mandan	Shoshone	
	Pawnee		
	Sioux		

Wigwams and Canoes Long ago, the eastern United States and Canada were covered with dense forests. These woodlands were the home of many animals. They offered a good food supply for the Indians of the region. Deer provided not only food but also buckskin for clothes and moccasins.

The forests also provided plenty of bark from tree trunks. The Indians used sheets of bark to cover their homes, called *wigwams*. They used birchbark to cover their canoes. These were so light they could easily be carried between rivers or past dangerous rapids. Women used birchbark to make boxes for storing and carrying food.

Indians even cooked in containers made of wood and bark. Of course, these would burn if placed over a fire. Instead, an Indian cook would fill the container with liquid, such as water or broth. Then she would drop in some stones that had been heated in a fire. More and more stones would be added, until the liquid boiled.

The woodland Indians were the first ones the English settlers met. Many of their words became part of our language. These include *opossum, raccoon, wampum, powwow, papoose,* and *tomahawk.*

In the Frozen North Much of northern Canada is cold and harsh. But small Indian groups managed to survive in this region, called the Subarctic.

Subarctic Indians lived almost entirely by hunting. They followed herds of caribou—large deer. This meant that they could not settle down in one place. During the winter—which lasts over eight months in the Subarctic—they traveled on snowshoes and pulled heavy loads on toboggans. The toboggans we know are made of wood. Wood is scarce in the Far North, so the Indians there used frozen animal skins. They also made houses of skins and poles. These could be carried easily and set in place quickly. In winter, such a shelter was often covered with snow for extra protection.

Indians of the frozen North used animal skins and fur for their clothing, too. For

Many woodland Indians hunted deer for food and made hides into clothing.

added warmth, they often sewed their moccasins to their leggings, the way we make children's pajamas.

Buffalo Hunters When you think of American Indians, you may imagine a warrior in a beautiful eagle-feather headdress. The tribes that honored their great men with this special headgear have become the most famous Indians of all. They were the buffalo hunters of the Great Plains. This grassy region stretches in a wide band from Texas north into Canada.

The Plains Indians grew some of their food and hunted various animals. But they relied mainly on the buffalo, which used to roam the plains in vast herds. The Indians ate buffalo meat, fresh or dried. They wore robes of buffalo fur. They used buffalo hides to make shields and boats. They drank from buffalo horns, burned buffalo droppings as fuel, and even brushed their hair with buffalo tongues. The Indians also covered their cone-shaped houses—called *tepees*—with buffalo hides.

The Plains Indians used buffalo hides to make tepees.

There were no horses in America until the Spaniards brought them in the 1500s. At first, the Plains Indians tracked buffalo on foot. Around 1600, they learned to use the horses that had been left by the Spanish. They could then hunt and fight more easily.

The Plains tribes were warlike and very proud. The eagle feathers men wore—and the designs they painted on their faces and tepees—indicated the great deeds they had done. (*See* **Sitting Bull.**)

Digging and Gathering The Indians of the western United States, too, were very good at adapting to their environment. In other words, they learned to make the most of what nature provided. Their land was not rich in animal life, so they ate small animals and insects, such as mice and grasshoppers. They did not grow crops. Instead, they dug roots and gathered all kinds of seeds, nuts, and berries. In California, acorns were plentiful. The Indians learned to soak, dry, and grind them to make a nutritious flour.

The diggers and gatherers of the West were nomads—wanderers. They built shelters of poles and grass, that could be moved easily. They made simple clothing—bark aprons and rabbit-fur cloaks. They also wove some of the finest baskets ever made anywhere in the world. They stored and carried food in these baskets. Some were so tightly woven that they could hold water. These could be used for cooking by the hot-stone method.

Totem-Pole Indians The Pacific coast, north of California, is a region of rain and fog. The land is forested with great cedars and other trees. The waters of the Pacific are full of fish, seals, and whales. Because of these natural resources, the Indians of this area lived very well.

Pacific coast Indians lived in villages and built large wooden houses. Several related families shared one house, with an area set aside for each one. In front of the house stood at least one totem pole. This was a big tree trunk, stripped of its bark and then carved and painted with designs of animals and birds. For each family group, certain animals or birds stood for famous ancestors and helpful spirits. The commonest figures included the bear, the whale, the raven, the wolf, and the eagle.

The plentiful wood of the Pacific coast was used for many other things as well. Men carved boats for travel and for hunting fish and sea mammals. They also made beautiful masks and drums for religious ceremonies, carved spoons and other tools, and shaped all sorts of containers. Women wove cedar bark into mats for sitting and sleeping and into fabric for clothes.

An unusual Pacific coast ceremony was the *potlatch*. A family would give a potlatch to celebrate an important occasion, such as a birth or a wedding. Many people were invited for days of dancing and feasting. But the most important part was giving away property—containers of fish oil, beautiful boxes, and colorful fringed blankets. The point of a potlatch was to show off a family's wealth and rank. The guests had to have potlatches of their own to avoid disgrace.

Desert Peoples Indians have lived for a long time in the Southwest—the hot, dry lands of Arizona and New Mexico. One group, the Pueblos, built multistory houses of stone and sun-dried brick. Each story was smaller than the one below it. The people had to climb a ladder, then go through a hole in the roof and climb down another ladder to get into their own "apartments."

Indians of the Northwest fished for salmon and are famous for their totem poles.

The Pueblos were good farmers. They raised corn, beans, squash, peppers, and cotton. They were peaceful Indians who honored their gods—Mother Earth and Father Sky—with many religious ceremonies. Much of their music and dancing was a kind of prayer to their gods, asking them to bring rain for their crops.

The Navaho were another Indian group of the Southwest. Each family lived in a separate house, called a *hogan*. After Europeans brought sheep and goats to America in the 1500s, the Navaho lived by herding. They also became famous for their beautiful weaving and their silver jewelry.

Conflict and Change When Europeans began settling in America, most of the Indians treated them as friends. For example, some Indians helped the Pilgrims in Massachusetts, and came to the first Thanksgiving celebration.

Trouble soon developed, however. One of the main problems was that Indians and whites had different ideas about land. Indians did not own land, either as individuals

Indians of the dry Southwest grew corn to eat and lived in adobe houses.

or as families. Instead, a tribe made use of a certain area, as we might use a campground. But white settlers wanted to own the Indians' land. They also wanted to change it forever by cutting down trees, building fences, and planting fields.

The settlers constantly pushed the Indians westward. They would "buy" thousands of acres of land for a few gallons of whiskey and some metal pots and rifles. They would force the Indians to move to new lands and tell them they could live there forever. But a few years later, the settlers would want these lands, too. (*See* **westward movement.**)

Some Indians gave up their lands peacefully. Others "went on the warpath" to defend what belonged to them. Famous Indian leaders such as Tecumseh and Geronimo fought long and hard to keep their old ways. (*See* **Tecumseh** and **Geronimo.**)

The Indians were hopelessly outnumbered by the whites. They did not have weapons as effective as those of the whites, either. But it was not just warfare that defeated the Indians. The settlers also brought invisible killers—diseases formerly unknown to the Indians—that cost many lives.

Finally, in the late 1800s, the United States government set aside areas of land called *reservations* for the Indians. Some reservations are large, but most have few natural resources. As a group, Indians today are poorer and have more illness than other Americans. They are free to leave their reservations, but most of them prefer to live among their own people.

Indians on an Arizona reservation discuss a land dispute, using a large map.

Today, there are about a million Indians in the United States—around the same number that lived in the United States in 1500. They are only a small part of the total U.S. population, but there are traces of their heritage everywhere. Many native animals have Indian names (chipmunk, moose). The names of many places in the United States are Indian names, including states (Massachusetts), cities (Chicago), rivers (the Mississippi), and mountains (the Alleghenies). Many of our roads began as Indian trails. The next time you wear moccasins, eat corn, or ride a toboggan, remember that you owe these things to American Indians.

See also **Indian Wars.**

Indian Wars

When Europeans first arrived in North America, there were about 1 million Indians already living there. As the newcomers moved west to settle new lands, the Indians tried to stop them. But the Indians were hopelessly outnumbered. In the end, they lost almost all the land that had been theirs for thousands of years.

British colonists settled Jamestown in Virginia in 1607. Other settlements followed. At

first, the colonists maintained peace with Chief Powhatan and the tribes he led. But in 1622, a new chief ordered his warriors to attack several settlements. More than 300 settlers died. Jamestown survived, but the Virginians and the Indians fought on and off for 12 more years.

The New England colonists, too, got along with the Indians at first. But by 1675, the Indians wanted the colonists to leave the Indians' land. Led by Metacomet, they began raiding settlements in southern New England. The Narraganset Indians helped the colonists defeat and kill Metacomet, but not before thousands of settlers were killed.

During the next 100 years, Britain and France fought for control of North America. Indian tribes often sided with the French against the British. But the British won. As more and more colonists came, the Indians were pushed farther west. There they often had to fight other tribes for land. (*See* **French and Indian War.**)

The colonists fought the British during both the Revolutionary War and the War of

"Custer's Last Stand," in which Custer and his men were killed. After the U.S. forced Indian peoples to surrender, many went to live on reservations.

1812. In these wars, the British paid the Indians to fight the colonists. Again the Indians hoped to stop the colonists, but again the Indians were disappointed. (*See* **Revolutionary War** and **War of 1812.**)

Throughout the first part of the 1800s, Americans fought to drive the Indians out of the Midwest. The great chief Tecumseh led several tribes in battle. They tried to stop the settlers from taking over what is now Indiana. But the Indians were defeated at the battle of Tippecanoe. Chief Black Hawk led Sauk and Fox warriors in the fight to keep their land in the upper Mississippi Valley. They, too, lost and were driven beyond the Mississippi River. (*See* **Tecumseh.**)

The Southeast—Georgia, Florida, Alabama, and Mississippi—had been the home of the Cherokee, Seminole, Chickasaw, Choctaw, and Creek tribes. When settlers wanted that land, the American government ordered the five tribes to move across the Mississippi River to territory in Oklahoma. U.S. Army troops marched them off on the long journey west. So many Indians suffered and died along the way that their long trek came to be called the "Trail of Tears."

The government promised that the land west of the Mississippi would belong to the Indians forever. But in the mid-1800s, settlers began to see it as good farmland. Gold and silver were discovered there, too.

This was the land of the Plains Indians—fierce warrior tribes like the Sioux, Cheyenne, and Apache. They lived by hunting huge herds of buffalo that roamed the plains. They did not want settlers turning their hunting grounds into farms. They did not want miners invading their deserts and mountains in search of gold and silver. They did not want miles of railroad track across their land.

The Indians were defeated again. Unlike the Indians in the East, the Plains Indians had horses. But the army built forts from which they could attack the Indians. Also, many tribes were starving because hunters had wiped out the buffalo herds.

Meanwhile, the American government was trying to force Indians to live only in certain areas, called *reservations*. The government again promised that this land would belong to the Indians forever.

The Sioux were given the Black Hills, in what is now South Dakota and Wyoming. This land was sacred to them, and they wanted to be left alone there. But then gold was discovered in the Black Hills, and the government ordered the Sioux out. This led to one of the most famous battles of the Indian Wars—the Battle of the Little Bighorn, or "Custer's Last Stand." Here, in 1876, Sioux and Cheyenne led by Sitting Bull and Crazy Horse wiped out a U.S. Army force. (*See* **Custer, George Armstrong.**)

To the south, in Arizona and New Mexico, Apaches led by Geronimo battled army troops, too. Through the 1880s, they continued to resist reservation life. But the fighting weakened them. In 1886, Geronimo was captured and forced to settle on a reservation. In 1890, Sitting Bull was killed. That same year, the Sioux staged a final uprising at Wounded Knee Creek in South Dakota. They were badly defeated by U.S. Army troops. With this defeat, the Indian Wars ended. (*See* **Geronimo** and **Sitting Bull.**)

Indonesia

Indonesia

Capital: Djakarta
Area: 735,268 square miles (1,909,344 square kilometers)
Population (1985): 173,103,000
Official language: Indonesian

Indonesia is a nation of more than 13,000 islands in southeastern Asia. The islands stretch about 3,200 miles (5,150 kilometers) from east to west along the equator.

Only four nations in the world have more people than Indonesia—China, India, the Soviet Union, and the United States. About half of the country's people live on the crowded island of Java. Djakarta, Indonesia's capital and largest city, is on Java. Many of Indonesia's other islands are small, and some of them have no people at all. There are about 60 active volcanoes on the islands. One of them, Krakatoa, killed about 36,000 people in 1883.

Indonesia has a warm, damp climate. There are huge rain forests in the lowlands. But in the mountains and highlands, the climate is cooler.

Indonesia has many natural resources. Rich soil and heavy rains provide huge crops of rice, sugarcane, fruits, and vegetables. Workers in Indonesia's rain forests harvest beautiful hardwoods and rubber. Most of these products are shipped to other parts of the world. Indonesia has few factories to process its own products.

The most valuable of Indonesia's resources is oil. Selling oil to other countries has brought much money to Indonesian businesses and government.

Indonesia is a country of many different cultures. More than 250 different languages are spoken in Indonesia. Most people are Muslims—followers of Islam. But many Indonesians follow local religions and Islam at the same time.

People in this Indonesian fishing village use sailboats for fishing and travel.

In an early cloth factory, women make cloth with the help of machines. They could make cloth much faster and less expensively than people could make it by hand.

The earliest settlers in the Indonesian Islands came from the mainland of Asia. In the 1600s, Arabs from the Middle East introduced the religion of Islam to the islands.

European traders began coming to Indonesia in the 1500s. They were looking for cinnamon and other spices that grow in the islands. In 1799, the Netherlands made Indonesia a colony. Indonesia finally became independent in 1945.

Indonesians are better off than many of their neighbors in Asia, because of the oil and other natural resources. But poverty, unemployment, and overcrowding are still major problems.

Industrial Revolution

In today's world, most strong nations rely on industry to produce wealth. This means that these nations are strong partly because workers in their factories produce a wide range of goods by machine. The United States, Canada, Japan, and most European countries are known as industrial nations.

For a long time, however, industry as we know it did not exist. Most people made a living by farming, by handicrafts, or by buying and selling goods. *Mass production*—making large numbers of things very quickly by machine—did not begin until the late 1700s.

When it did, it made such a difference in people's lives that the change is known as the Industrial Revolution.

The Industrial Revolution began in England. It started in the field of textiles—the making of cloth. For years, the English made fine woolen cloth by spinning and weaving in their homes. Then, machines were invented that could spin and weave much faster. These were too big for houses, so they were put in factories. At first, machines were run by waterpower. Later, steam engines were used.

Businessmen soon built factories all over England. They opened mines to dig the coal that fueled the steam engines. Railroads—also run by steam—soon crisscrossed the land. Huge furnaces produced iron and steel for building the machines and railroads. The Industrial Revolution spread to other countries, especially France, Germany, and the United States.

The Industrial Revolution brought rapid progress in many industries. In transportation, the railroad was followed by the steamboat, the automobile, and the airplane. In communication, the telegraph, telephone, radio, and television made it possible to send messages around the world in seconds. Many discoveries have also been made in the fields of chemistry and electricity.

In the early 1900s, some children had to work every day, even before age ten.

The Industrial Revolution had its grim side. Factory work was often hard, dangerous, and poorly paid. Before child-labor laws were passed, young children worked 10 or 12 hours a day for a few cents. Families lived crowded together in miserable slums.

But industrial progress also led to better medical care and to many inventions that made everyday life easier. Today, most nations that have not yet gone through an industrial revolution are trying to do so.

infection

Your body is constantly battling millions of tiny invaders. Most can be seen only with a microscope. But when they invade the body and begin to reproduce, they cause infection.

The invaders include bacteria, viruses, fungi, protists, and parasitic worms. Bacteria cause diseases such as typhoid fever, pneumonia, and botulism. Bacteria can also infect open wounds. Viruses cause diseases such as the common cold and the flu. Fungus diseases include ringworm and athlete's foot. Protists cause malaria and African

sleeping sickness. Parasitic worms include hookworms and tapeworms. (*See* **bacteria; virus; fungus; protist;** and **parasite.**)

The body's white blood cells capture and destroy invading bacteria and viruses. The body also produces *antibodies* to fight infection. Fever may be another way the body fights infection. (*See* **antibody; blood;** and **fever.**)

You can help prevent infections by eating well, getting lots of rest, and washing often. You should also be vaccinated against serious diseases. (*See* **vaccine.**)

When you are sick, you can help stop the spread of infection by not exposing others to your illness.

See also **disease and sickness.**

In this photo from an electron microscope, human white blood cells attack an invader much larger than themselves.

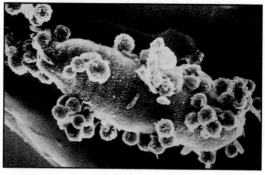

influenza

Influenza is a contagious disease caused by a virus. It is commonly known as "the flu." Symptoms of the flu include a sore throat, cough, chills, fever, aching muscles, and loss of appetite.

Flu epidemics often occur in winter and early spring. Healthy people are exposed to the virus in droplets from the coughs or sneezes of infected people. In this way, the virus may spread to entire cities, states, or continents in a short time. Some epidemics have spread around the world.

The only treatment for influenza is bed rest. Medicine can control the fever and reduce the pain. Vaccination can help prevent influenza. But immunity lasts only a few months, so it is necessary to be vaccinated each year. (*See* **vaccine**.)

Influenza by itself is not usually a serious disease. But it can lower the body's resistance to other, more serious diseases, such as bronchitis and pneumonia. Older people and infants have a higher risk of developing these diseases. But antibiotics have made them less dangerous than they used to be. In 1918, before antibiotics were developed, an influenza epidemic killed millions of people around the world.

See also **antibiotic; virus;** and **disease and sickness.**

infrared light

In 1800, the astronomer Sir William Herschel made an interesting discovery. He held a thermometer so it was in the colors of the *spectrum*—the rainbow formed by sunlight passing through a prism. He found that red light was warmer than the light passing through other colors. But when he held the thermometer below the red, where he could see nothing, the temperature was still higher. Herschel had discovered a form of light "below the red." This light was named infrared light. *Infra* means "below."

In this infrared photo, red areas are warm, while green and blue areas are cooler.

Infrared light, like visible light, is a kind of electromagnetic wave. Of the colors we see, red has the longest wavelength. Infrared waves are longer than waves of red light. We cannot see infrared light, but if it is strong enough, we feel it as heat.

Every object gives off some infrared waves. Some devices use a special film to get a picture of these waves. This picture is called a *thermal image*. A thermal image might be used to show the heat in a house during the winter. If warm air is escaping through a leak, the leak will show up in the picture. Thermal images are used by the military to "see" at night. Doctors use them to locate some diseases. Satellites use them to record changes in vegetation on Earth.

See also **light.**

ink

Ink is liquid used for writing and printing. Inks come in every color. Historians believe that both the Chinese and Egyptians started making ink around 2500 B.C.

Ink called *India ink* is made from carbon mixed with a vegetable glue or gum, shaped into cakes or sticks, and dried. To get a liquid, the dry ink is rubbed with water. This ink can stay dark for thousands of years.

The American colonists made black ink by mixing iron, tannic acid from oak trees, and water, wine, or vinegar. After a few years, some of these inks would fade away. Others had so much acid that they eventually burned lacy holes in paper.

Today, inks made from dyes, and other substances go into ballpoint and fiber-tip pens. Typewriters and computer printers use ink on a long ribbon. *Indelible inks* —inks that will not wash out—are used for marking laundry. *Printing inks* are made to dry quickly, to keep them from smearing as paper runs through a printing press.

You can make "invisible ink" from lemon juice or vinegar. To read the message, hold the paper near a candle flame or light bulb. The warmth will turn the writing brown.

insect

There are almost a million known kinds of insects—more than all other kinds of animals combined. Insects come in many shapes, colors, and sizes. They live in almost every kind of environment. They include ants, flies, butterflies, fleas, beetles, wasps, and bees. These creatures may seem very different from one another, but they all share certain features.

The Body of an Insect The tough covering on the outside of an insect is its skeleton. It is called an *exoskeleton,* because it is outside. The exoskeleton gives the body its shape. Like a suit of armor, it protects the soft body parts inside. It also keeps the body from drying out.

The body of an adult insect is divided into three parts—head, thorax, and abdomen.

The head is the front part. On it are the eyes, a pair of antennae, and the mouth parts. Most insects have two large *compound eyes.* A compound eye is a cluster of many single lenses. Compound eyes make it easy for an insect to see even the slightest movement.

The antennae may look feathery or they may look like threads. On the antennae are various sense organs. The antennae of blood-sucking insects sense temperature. This helps the insects find warm-blooded animals. Moths use their antennae as noses, to smell chemicals given off by moths of the opposite sex. Ants use their antennae to communicate. When two ants tap each other's antennae, they are "talking."

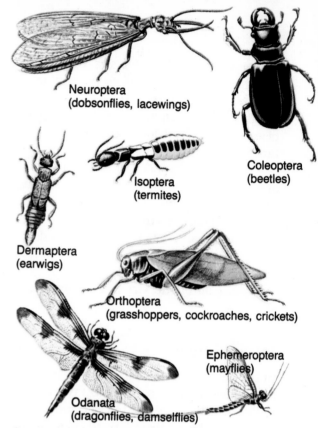

Neuroptera
(dobsonflies, lacewings)

Coleoptera
(beetles)

Isoptera
(termites)

Dermaptera
(earwigs)

Orthoptera
(grasshoppers, cockroaches, crickets)

Ephemeroptera
(mayflies)

Odanata
(dragonflies, damselflies)

Some main insect families. There are thousands of different kinds in one family.

Insects have different kinds of mouthparts, depending on what they eat. Some insects have chewing mouthparts. They eat solid foods, such as leaves and other insects. Some insects have mouthparts shaped like a soda straw. They sip nectar from flowers. Insects that suck blood have sharp, tube-like mouthparts that can pierce skin.

The thorax is the middle part of the body. It contains the powerful muscles needed for moving the wings and legs. Most kinds of insects have two pairs of wings. But some have only one pair, and a few have no wings at all. All insects have three pairs of legs—six legs in all. Spiders and ticks are not insects. They have eight legs.

Insect legs come in many shapes. Grasshoppers have legs designed for jumping. Water beetles have oarlike legs to help them swim. Water striders walk on the surfaces of ponds. Their legs are covered with hairs that prevent them from sinking.

The abdomen is at the end of the insect's body. It contains the heart. It also contains

Insects have three pairs of legs. On a grasshopper, one set of legs is very long.

Parts of an Insect

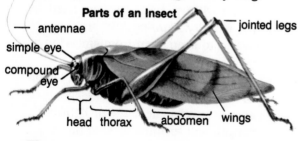

antennae

jointed legs

simple eye

compound eye

head   thorax   abdomen   wings

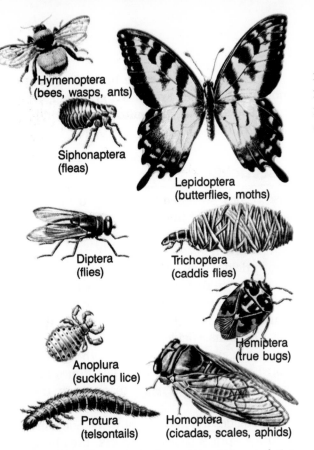

Hymenoptera
(bees, wasps, ants)

Siphonaptera
(fleas)

Lepidoptera
(butterflies, moths)

Diptera
(flies)

Trichoptera
(caddis flies)

Hemiptera
(true bugs)

Anoplura
(sucking lice)

Protura
(telsontails)

Homoptera
(cicadas, scales, aphids)

nymphs of the grasshopper and dragonfly, for example, do not have wings. The nymphs must grow two pairs of wings before they become adults.

Complete metamorphosis has four stages —egg, larva, pupa, and adult. The larva that hatches from the egg does not look at all like an adult. Butterflies and moths are insects that go through complete metamorphosis. A butterfly or moth larva is called a *caterpillar.* It looks like a worm. It does not have the adult's wings or colors. The caterpillar is a big eater. The more it eats, the bigger it grows. After it has eaten all it can, it goes into the pupa stage. It makes a hard skin—the pupal case. Unlike most insect larvae, moth caterpillars spin a *cocoon* of threadlike materials. The cocoon hardens into a pupal case as the pupa inside changes into a moth.

An insect's exoskeleton cannot grow. So whenever an insect grows or changes its shape, it must *molt*—shed its exoskeleton. It then grows a new, bigger exoskeleton. Some kinds of insects molt as many as 30 times before reaching their full adult size.

Insects and People Many insects are helpful to people. Some pollinate plants we grow for food. They carry pollen from one flower to another. Without this work, many plants—such as apple, pear, and cherry trees—cannot make fruits and seeds.

the digestive, respiratory, excretory, and the reproductive systems.

Stages of Life All insects hatch from eggs. In a few kinds, the young look exactly like adults, except that they are much smaller. But in most kinds of insects, the young do not look like adults. They have to undergo *metamorphosis*—a change of form—before they become adults. There are just two kinds of insect metamorphosis—incomplete and complete.

Incomplete metamorphosis has three stages—egg, nymph, and adult. The nymph hatches from the egg. It may look something like the adult. But as a nymph, not all of the insect's adult body parts are complete. The

Many insects have four life stages—egg, larva, pupa, and adult. A moth larva is called a caterpillar. Its pupa is called a *cocoon.*

male

adults

female

pupa
(cocoon)

larva
(caterpillar)

egg masses

Bees produce honey, which people eat. They also make beeswax, which is used in making polishes, candles, and other products. Silkworms—the larvae of certain kinds of moths—spin cocoons of silk. People unroll the cocoons and use the silk to make fabric. The dried bodies of cochineals—insects related to mealybugs—are used to make a brilliant red dye.

Other useful insects are *scavengers*. They eat dead plants and animals. Without these insects, dead bodies would take much longer to decay.

Many insects are useful because they are *predators*. They eat harmful insects. But other insects eat farm crops, flower gardens, and even whole forests. Some feed on foods and grains kept in homes and storage buildings. Clothes moths and carpet beetles ruin clothing and carpets. Mosquitoes, bedbugs, and gnats bite people. Other insects bite cattle and other animals raised by people.

Some insects carry germs that cause disease. When the insects bite people or animals, the germs enter the victims' blood. Malaria, yellow fever, and sleeping sickness are among the diseases carried by insects.

People use chemicals called *insecticides* to kill insects. Often, these chemicals kill good insects as well as harmful insects. The chemicals can also hurt birds, earthworms, other helpful animals, people, and the soil.

A silkworm makes a cocoon of fine threads. People have learned to unwind the thread and make it into silk cloth.

See also ant; bee; beetle; butterflies and moths; caterpillar; firefly; fly; grasshopper; insecticide; larva; mosquitoes and gnats; and termite.

insecticide

Insecticides are chemicals used to kill insects. People use insecticides to kill insects that eat plants, spread disease, and live in and around homes.

Insecticides may be sprayed directly on the insects, or on their food or nests. Sometimes insecticides are mixed with an insect's food. Some ant and cockroach traps work this way. Other insecticides make fumes that poison the insects. Mothballs or moth crystals stored with clothing do this. The fumes kill any moths or moth eggs that are in the clothing.

Insecticides kill in different ways. Some insecticide sprays clog the insects' breathing tubes. Other chemicals make the insects' nervous systems stop working. Some insecticides make it impossible for the insects to reproduce.

Plants can make substances that poison insects. Nicotine from tobacco plants is used to poison insects that suck on plants. Pyrethrum is found in chrysanthemum flowers. It is used on flies and cabbage worms. Most insecticides are chemicals made in laboratories. Chlordane, DDT, carbaryl, and TEPP are some of the human-made insecticides.

DDT was once widely used to control insect pests. But DDT lasts a long time in the environment. It does not break down into harmless chemicals. It can get into the water system and the food chain, passing from one living thing to another. In the 1950s and 1960s, condors, eagles, and other birds at the top of the food chain got a lot of DDT in their food. The DDT made the birds lay eggs with soft shells. When the birds sat on their eggs, the eggs broke, so no young birds hatched. In the United States, DDT is now used only in special cases where other insecticides will not work. It is still used in some

Insecticides are chemicals that can kill insect pests. They can be sprayed on food crops (above) or used indoors (right). Insecticides can be dangerous if misused.

other countries, however. (*See* **food chain** and **Carson, Rachel.**)

Most insecticides are used in agriculture. Farmers can spread insecticides over large fields by dropping the chemicals from a small airplane called a *crop duster.* Home gardeners also use insecticides to keep their fruits, vegetables, and flowers free of insects.

Insecticides help control insects on farms and in our homes. But some of these chemicals are poisonous to animals and people, too. Insecticides should be used carefully.

insurance

Insurance is a way for people to protect themselves from expensive bills caused by accidents, storms, fire, sickness, or death. The first insurance company in the United States was started by Benjamin Franklin in 1752.

Insurance companies provide insurance according to agreements called *policies.* The person who buys the insurance pays the insurance company a fee called a *premium.* In return, if a disaster listed in the policy happens, the insurance company will pay the person who has the insurance.

Health insurance is the most common kind of insurance. It pays a large part of

hospital and doctors' bills. Some policies also cover medicines, ambulance rides, and nursing care.

Auto insurance is very common, too. If a car is damaged or stolen, auto insurance will help pay to fix or replace it. Most states require that automobiles be insured for the damage they could do to people or property they might hit.

People can also buy life insurance. For this kind of insurance policy, the insured person names someone to receive the amount of money named in the policy when the insured person dies.

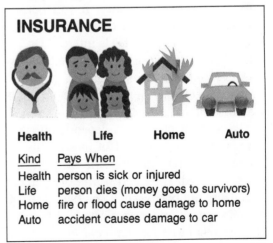

INSURANCE

Health	Life	Home	Auto

Kind	Pays When
Health	person is sick or injured
Life	person dies (money goes to survivors)
Home	fire or flood cause damage to home
Auto	accident causes damage to car

intelligence

Intelligence is the ability to learn, understand, and reason. Each of us is strong in some kinds of intelligence and not as strong in other kinds. One person may find it easy to memorize facts. Someone else may be quick to understand how machines work. A person may be able to learn a foreign language easily but have trouble solving math problems. Some people learn faster than most people, or remember things longer.

Scientists have developed tests to measure intelligence. They figure out a person's *intelligence quotient*—IQ—by seeing how well the person solves problems designed for his or her age group and older. But some scientists say that these tests are unfair because they measure only certain kinds of intelligence. For example, intelligence tests do not measure a person's mechanical skill, artistic talent, or musical ability.

How well children do on intelligence tests may be connected to the way they were brought up—or even how they were fed! Scientists know that children who do not get the right vitamins, minerals, and other important substances in food may have trouble developing their full intelligence.

See also **learning.**

interest

Interest is what a person, bank, or company pays for the use of money. If you borrow money, you usually must pay a fee for the use of that money. The fee is interest. On the other hand, if you put your money in a savings account at a bank, the bank pays you for the use of your money. This payment is also interest.

The amount of interest depends on three things—the total amount of money, the interest rate, and the amount of time the money is used. The *interest rate* is a percent of the amount borrowed. If you borrow $100 for one year at an interest rate of 8 percent, the interest owed for that year is $8. If you

borrow $100 for two years at a rate of 8 percent, you will have to pay $16 interest—$8 for each year.

Interest on savings accounts is usually paid several times during the year. A bank may pay daily, monthly, or every three months. The bank pays you interest by adding it to your savings account. This way, the interest will also earn interest. This is called *compound interest.*

See also **bank.**

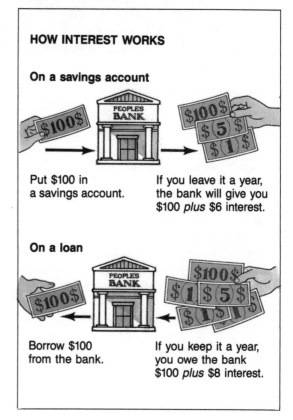

HOW INTEREST WORKS

On a savings account

Put $100 in a savings account.

If you leave it a year, the bank will give you $100 *plus* $6 interest.

On a loan

Borrow $100 from the bank.

If you keep it a year, you owe the bank $100 *plus* $8 interest.

international date line

The international date line is an imaginary line down the middle of the Pacific Ocean. If it is noon on Monday on the east side of the line, it is noon on Tuesday on the west side.

Why do we need such a line? Imagine that you could start just west of the date line and fly westward around the world in a single day. There are 24 time zones in the world. Each time you move from one to another, you set your watch back an hour.

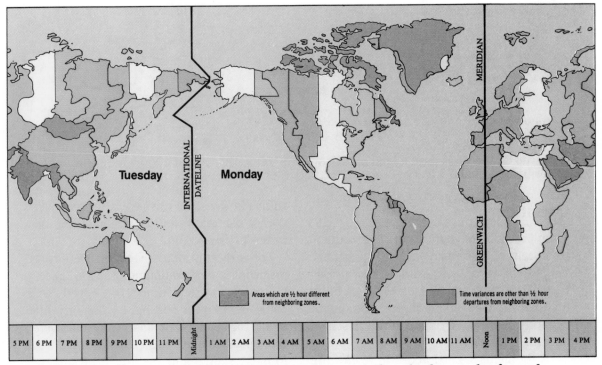

When crossing the international date line going west, move the calendar one day forward.
When crossing the line going east, move the calendar one day backward.

When you get near the date line at the end of your trip, you have traveled almost 24 hours. But you have set your clock back 23 times, so it is still between noon and one o'clock on the same day! How could an all-day and all-night trip take no time at all?

When you cross the international date line, you set your watch back one more time to 12:01. But you move your calendar ahead one day. So the trip has taken one day, even though the time on your watch stayed between noon and one o'clock.

If there were no international date line, you could travel west around the world and keep the calendar from changing. This would be confusing. After one day's travel, it would be Monday to you, but it would be Tuesday to everyone else!

See also **latitude and longitude.**

intestine

The intestine is the part of the digestive system that food passes through after leaving the stomach. It consists of a small intestine and a large intestine. The *small intestine* is a narrow, muscular tube about 7 meters (23 feet) long. The *large intestine* is wider and about 1.5 meters (5 feet) long.

Although digestion begins in the mouth and stomach, most of the process takes place in the small intestine. Two glands—the liver and the pancreas—release digestive fluids into the small intestine. Tiny glands in the walls of the small intestine produce other digestive juices. The digestive juices break down food particles into small molecules. (*See* **gland** and **liver.**)

The walls of the small intestine are lined with millions of tiny fingerlike projections called *villi.* They help absorb molecules of digested food into the bloodstream. What reaches the lower end of the small intestine is only water and waste materials.

The large intestine takes water from this waste material and then eliminates the solid wastes.

See also **digestion** and **human body.**

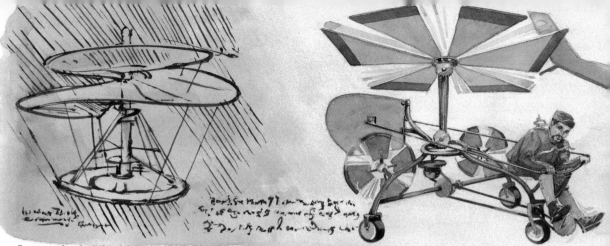

Leonardo da Vinci imagined a kind of helicopter in 1483 (left). About 1900, inventors began trying to build a real helicopter. By 1930, they had succeeded (right).

invention

From the moment your *alarm clock* sounds, you begin to use thousands of inventions. You brush your teeth with a *toothbrush,* bathe in a *bathtub,* and dress in clothing that has *zippers* and *buttons.* You might turn on the *radio.* Perhaps you ride to school on your *bicycle.*

All the items named above in *italics* are human inventions. An invention is any new device or process developed to solve a particular problem.

Many animals build things. Beavers build dams, ants dig tunnels, and birds weave nests. But nearly all animals build the same things in the same way year after year. They do not use reason to invent something new to meet their needs.

The earliest human inventions were based on people's observations of natural objects. Our ancestors saw that sharp-edged rocks could be used for cutting. So they invented stone tools and weapons. They discovered that sparks make fire, so they invented ways to make sparks and use fire. They saw that logs and round rocks will roll. They went on to invent the wheel.

Unlike other animals, humans keep improving their inventions. They also use old inventions as a starting place for coming up with new inventions. People did not just sit

IMPORTANT INVENTIONS SINCE 1800

Date	Invention	Inventor and Country
1804	**steam locomotive**	Richard Trevithick, England
1807	**practical steamboat**	Robert Fulton, United States
1836	**telegraph**	Samuel F.B. Morse, United States
1846	**sewing machine**	Elias Howe, United States
1849	**safety pin**	Walter Hunt, United States
1866	**pedal bicycle**	Pierre Lallement, France
1867	**dynamite**	Alfred Nobel, Sweden
1876	**telephone**	Alexander Graham Bell, United States
1877	**phonograph**	Thomas Alva Edison, United States
1879	**incandescent light**	Thomas Alva Edison, United States
1885	**gasoline engine**	G. Daimler and K. Benz, Germany
1888	**box camera for home use**	George Eastman, United States
1889	**movie camera and projector**	Thomas Alva Edison, United States
1893	**zipper**	Whitcomb L. Judson, United States
1895	**radio transmission**	Guglielmo Marconi, Italy
1903	**airplane**	Wright brothers, United States
1923	**television**	Vladimir Zworykin, United States
1930	**jet engine for airplane**	Frank Whittle, England
1960	**laser**	Theodore H. Maiman, United States

around their fires keeping warm while they sharpened stones. They invented other uses for fire. Fire could be used to melt the metals in rocks. Once people knew how to get metals, they invented ways to shape, harden, and sharpen the metals. If you think about all the things humans have invented, it is easy to understand why we are called "the inventing animal."

Ideas can be inventions, just as things can. Language, numbers, and writing are inventions. Some people say that the number 0 is among our greatest inventions. Language, numbers, and writing are probably the most important inventions. People use them to communicate their inventions to others.

We do not know the names of many early inventors. But we know the names of many recent inventors. We know that Benjamin Franklin invented the lightning rod and bifocal eyeglasses, and that Alexander Graham Bell invented the telephone. Often, the person given credit for an invention is not the person who first thought of it or built it, but the person who made the invention work best. For example, Thomas Edison did not make the first light bulb, and Robert Fulton did not make the first steamboat. But they invented light bulbs and steamboats that worked better than the earlier ones.

Some complex devices are the result of many inventions and inventors. Different people invented the automobile engine, the starter, the brakes, the tires, and so forth. When Karl Benz made what is often called the "first" automobile, many of the parts of a modern car were not yet invented.

Today, when a new invention is created, the inventor gets a government *patent* on the invention. A patent says the inventor owns the invention. That means that no one can copy or make the invention without the permission of the owner. The patent is good for only a limited time—17 years in the United States. By then, the inventor should have made a fair profit from the invention. After that, other people can freely use the invention.

See also **automobile; bicycle; Fulton, Robert; Bell, Alexander Graham;** and **Edison, Thomas Alva.**

invertebrate, *see* animal

iodine

Years ago, everyone knew iodine as a red-brown liquid that you put on cuts. Because the liquid stung, children did not like "iodine." But the red-brown liquid was not iodine. It was alcohol in which iodine was dissolved. The alcohol caused the sting. Today, most people use other antiseptics.

Iodine is an element. By itself at room temperature, it is a solid. It is not a metal, but forms small, dark crystals. When you heat the iodine crystals, they do not melt. Instead, they turn into a beautiful violet gas. The name *iodine* comes from the Greek word for "violet."

Our bodies need iodine. It is part of the hormone produced by the thyroid, a gland in the neck. The hormone controls how fast our body changes food to energy. If there is not enough iodine, the thyroid gland grows very large. This condition is called *goiter*. A tiny amount of iodine is put into table salt to prevent goiter.

Goiter is not common among people who live near the sea and eat lots of seafood. Seafood and seaweed picks up iodine from ocean water. Iodine was discovered in 1811 by a scientist looking for important chemicals in seaweed.

Iowa

Capital: Des Moines
Area: 56,275 square miles (145,752 square kilometers) (25th-largest state)
Population (1980): 2,913,808 (1985): about 2,884,000 (29th-largest state)
Became a state: December 28, 1846 (29th state)

Corn is Iowa's most important crop. Most of the corn is fed to farm animals.

Iowa is a state in the midwestern United States. Its name is an Indian word that means "beautiful land." The land is indeed beautiful. It is also good farmland. Iowa has more good farmland than any other state. One-tenth of the U.S. food supply is produced in Iowa.

Land Iowa's northern and southern boundaries are almost straight, but its eastern and western borders are squiggly. That is because the Mississippi River forms the eastern border and the Big Sioux and Missouri rivers form the western border.

Millions of years ago, most of Iowa was covered by giant ice sheets called *glaciers*. When the glaciers melted, they left behind rolling plains and fertile soil. Cold winters and hot summers bring enough moisture to grow corn and many other crops. More corn is grown in Iowa than in any other state. Most of it is fed to hogs and cattle. But corn is also used for making many products. In fact, more than 2,400 supermarket products are made with some part of the corn kernel or cob! Corn oil is often used for cooking. Corn syrup sweetens most soft drinks and candies. Gravies and sauces are often thickened with cornstarch. Some corn is grown for popping. The largest popcorn factory in the world is in Sioux City, Iowa.

Iowa farmers also grow soybeans, oats, and hay. They raise cattle, hogs, turkeys, and other livestock. About three-fourths of the

farmers' income comes from selling their livestock, not from selling the crops they grow.

People Almost half of the people in Iowa live in rural areas. The rest live in towns and small cities. Most of the people in Iowa are great-great-grandchildren of European immigrants. Some Iowans still keep European customs.

The population of Iowa has not grown very much since 1970. Times have been difficult for farm families, and many people have moved to other states.

The biggest city in the state is Des Moines, the capital. It is a trade center for the surrounding farms. A second large city is Davenport, on the Mississippi River. Davenport is one of the "Quad-Cities," four cities that cluster together on the river. The other three cities are just across the river, in Illinois.

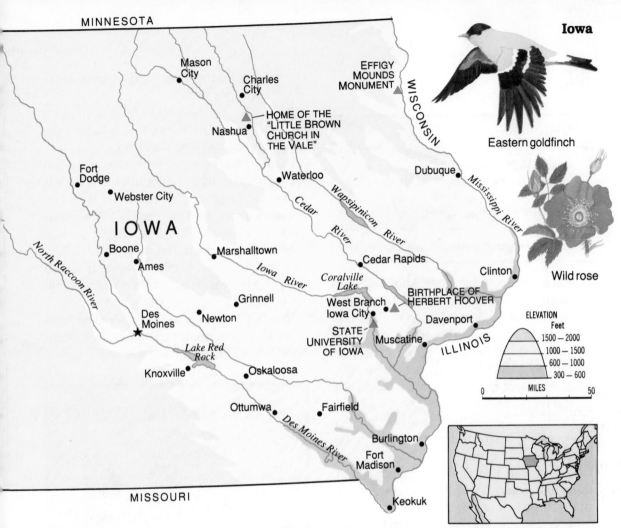

MINNESOTA

Iowa

Mason City

Charles City

EFFIGY MOUNDS MONUMENT

WISCONSIN

Eastern goldfinch

HOME OF THE "LITTLE BROWN CHURCH IN THE VALE"

Nashua

Fort Dodge

Webster City

Waterloo

Dubuque

Mississippi River

Cedar River

Wapsipinicon River

I O W A

Boone

Ames

Marshalltown

Iowa River

Coralville Lake

Cedar Rapids

Clinton

Wild rose

Grinnell

West Branch

Iowa City

BIRTHPLACE OF HERBERT HOOVER

Davenport

Des Moines

Newton

North Raccoon River

STATE UNIVERSITY OF IOWA

Muscatine

ILLINOIS

Lake Red Rock

ELEVATION Feet

1500 — 2000

1000 — 1500

600 — 1000

300 — 600

Knoxville

Oskaloosa

0   MILES   50

Ottumwa

Fairfield

Des Moines River

Burlington

Fort Madison

▲ Historical Sites and Points of Interest

MISSOURI

Keokuk

History A group of prehistoric Indians called Mound Builders lived in Iowa about 1,000 years ago. They heaped up earth and stones to make hills, mostly for burial grounds. Some were shaped like animals. Many of the mounds are protected in Effigy Mounds National Monument.

The first Europeans to visit the area were probably the French explorers Jacques Marquette and Louis Jolliet. In 1673, they paddled down the Mississippi River in canoes. They claimed the area to the west of the river for France. For the next 150 years, there were many French and Indian explorers and hunters in the area. The United States bought the land from France in 1803, as part of the Louisiana Purchase. Early settlers fought many bloody battles against the Indians. Iowa became a territory in 1838 and a state in 1846. (*See* **Louisiana Purchase**.)

One of the most interesting groups of people in Iowa are those in the Amana colonies. These religious people came from Germany. They moved first to New York and then, in 1855, to Iowa. For nearly 100 years, all the buildings and other possessions in Amana belonged to the group, not to individuals. The Amana colonists sold furniture, woolen cloth, and other goods to people outside the community. Today, they own a well-known company that makes refrigerators, freezers, and microwave ovens.

Every August, Iowans gather in Des Moines for the famous Iowa State Fair. Half a million people come to see the exhibits. Iowans compete in contests that show the importance of agriculture in the state. Adults win prizes for growing the best corn or making the best jelly. Teenagers win prizes for raising the best pigs or calves.

81

Iran

Capital: Teheran
Area: 636,293 square miles (1,026,279 square kilometers)
Population (1985): 45,191,000
Official language: Persian (Farsi)

Iran is a large country in the Middle East. It is about one-fourth the size of the United States both in land area and in population.

On the west, Iran borders Iraq and Turkey. To the north, it faces the Soviet Union. Its eastern border is with Afghanistan and Pakistan. Iran faces three seas—the Caspian Sea on the north, and the Persian Gulf and Gulf of Oman on the south. Iran's location has made it a crossroads for trade routes between Asia and Europe.

Most of Iran is covered by rugged mountains and desert. These regions receive less than 10 inches of rain a year—too little to grow crops. But Iran has underground irrigation canals to bring water to its crops.

Most Iranians live in mountain valleys in the northwestern part of the country and along the shores of the Caspian Sea. These regions receive more rain and produce most of the country's food.

Iran is among the world's leading producers of oil and natural gas. Iran's largest deposits are near the Persian Gulf.

Iran has long been a center of civilization. For many centuries the country was known as Persia. Beginning in the 500s B.C., the Persians built a great empire. They conquered many peoples, from Egypt in the southwest to India in the east.

In the 300s B.C., warlike peoples from the west and the east invaded Persia. But Persia remained a center of learning and art.

In A.D. 641, Persia was conquered by Arab armies, who brought the Islamic religion. Soon, all of Persia followed the new religion.

This mosque in Yazd is one of Iran's many beautiful places of worship.

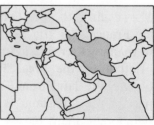

Ever since, the region has been important to Islamic culture.

Iran became independent in the 1920s. Its ruler, the shah, worked to unify the many tribes living in Iran. He modernized industry and made people dress in European clothes.

Then, in 1979, Islamic leaders led by the Ayatollah Khomeini overthrew the government. They made new laws based on Islamic laws and customs. The new laws allowed people to vote, but gave Khomeini great power. Islamic leaders continue to rule Iran. Since 1980, Iran has been at war with Iraq over land and religious issues.

A busy street in Baghdad, the capital of Iraq.

Iraq

Capital: Baghdad
Area: 167,924 square miles (434,923 square kilometers)
Population (1985): about 15,507,000
Official language: Arabic

Iraq is an Arab country in the Middle East. It has a small shoreline on the Persian Gulf. The Tigris and Euphrates rivers flow through Iraq's center. Long ago, the area was known as Mesopotamia—"Land Between the Rivers." The world's earliest civilizations began here 5,000 years ago. Today, Iraq is known as an oil-rich country.

Most of Iraq's people are Arabs. They live in cities in the fertile valley between the Tigris and Euphrates. Baghdad, the capital city, is on the Tigris. Another large group, the Kurds, live in the mountains in the northeast. Both the Arabs and Kurds are Muslims, followers of Islam. Village people live in small stone or mud-brick houses. City people often live in modern apartment buildings or houses.

Some Iraqis are *nomads*—people who roam the mountains and desert with their animals. Others work in the oil industry.

Iraqi farmers grow mainly barley and dates. More dates are grown in Iraq than anywhere else in the world. Next to oil, dates are Iraq's most important export product.

In 1980, Iraq and neighboring Iran went to war over a disagreement about land. Much of the money Iraq has made from oil has been used to fight the war with Iran.

Ireland

Capital: Dublin
Area: 27,136 square miles (70,282 square kilometers)
Population (1985): 3,588,000
Official languages: English, Gaelic

Ireland is a country that takes up more than three-fourths of an island in northwestern Europe. The rest of the island is occupied by Northern Ireland, a part of the United Kingdom. The entire island, with its green pastures and rolling green hills, is often called the "Emerald Isle."

ELEVATION
Feet
2000 — 5000
1000 — 2000
0 — 1000

MILES
0   100

NORTH ATLANTIC OCEAN

Donegal Bay

NORTHERN IRELAND (U.K.)

Sligo

IRELAND

Drogheda

Athlone

Galway Bay — Galway

Shannon River

Dublin

Dun Laoghaire

Limerick

Barrow River

Blackwater River   Waterford

Killarney

Cork   Cobh

Wexford

Rosslare

Skibbereen

Irish Sea

Land Ireland is farther north than the continental United States, but temperatures there hardly ever fall below freezing. The Gulf Stream—a warm current in the Atlantic Ocean—brings Ireland warm winds and plenty of rain.

Much of the land is hilly and rocky, but there are also regions of rich soil. Many Irish live in the countryside and grow some of their own food. Bays, coves, and inlets along the coasts provide harbors for fishermen. For many Irish, fishing is a way of life. Ireland is also known for its crystal glassware and handcrafts.

History About 2,000 years ago, the island was settled by the Celts, who brought the ancient Gaelic language. Some Irish still use Irish, a form of Gaelic. (*See* **Celts**.)

In the 400s, a bishop named Patrick brought Christianity to Ireland. Patrick was born in western Britain. When he was young, he was captured by slave traders and sold as a slave in Ireland. After several years, he escaped, but he returned later as a missionary. St. Patrick's Day, March 17, is celebrated in his honor.

Beginning in the 1100s, the English got a foothold in Ireland. For centuries, Ireland struggled to remain free of English rule. In

Ireland's green countryside and seacoasts are famous. An ancient castle is a reminder of the country's long history.

1541, King Henry VIII of England forced the Irish to declare him their king. Irish land was given to English settlers. Thousands of Englishmen and Scots came to Ireland. The Irish fought back, but the English were too strong.

The Irish also had to fight poverty and hunger. Potatoes were the main food. But in the mid-1800s, a disease killed nearly all the potatoes. More than 750,000 people starved. Millions of Irish had to leave their country. Many moved to the United States. Others went to Great Britain, Canada, or Australia.

In 1921, Ireland finally won independence from England. But Ireland's six northern counties remain part of the United Kingdom. They form Northern Ireland. Many people think Ireland should be united, and there is often violence in the North over this issue.

The Irish government has helped start new industries and encourages tourists to visit Ireland. Visitors enjoy the scenery, lively music, and friendly people. The Irish are great storytellers and have produced many famous writers, such as William Butler Yeats, Sean O'Casey, and James Joyce.

iron

Iron is one of the most common elements on Earth. Today, iron is used more than any other metal. Most metal tools contain iron. Automobiles and skyscrapers are built on frames that contain iron. The metals in furniture and fences may contain iron.

Although iron is so common, you probably have never seen pure iron. Pure iron is a silver-white metal that can easily be shaped by hammering. Wrought iron is the closest thing to pure iron. Wrought iron contains a very small amount of carbon. To shape this iron, a blacksmith heats it and hammers it.

Another common form of iron is cast iron. Cast iron contains much more carbon than does wrought iron. This makes cast iron so hard that it cannot be shaped by heating and hammering. Instead, it is shaped by pouring the melted iron into molds.

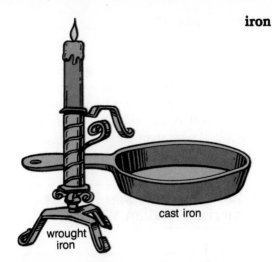

cast iron

wrought iron

Wrought iron is shaped when red-hot.
Cast iron is melted and poured into a mold.

The most important use of iron is in making steel. Steel is an alloy made of iron and other metals. It contains more carbon than does wrought iron, but less than cast iron. (*See* **alloy** and **steel**.)

The Hittites from the Middle East first learned how to make wrought iron in large quantities about 3,200 years ago. About 1,000 years later, the Chinese developed cast iron. Before these inventions, weapons and tools were made from bronze, a blend of tin and copper.

Iron is stronger than bronze, and easier to find than tin or copper. Using iron plows, people tilled more land and produced more food. They made iron saws, hatchets, hammers, and cutting tools for building wooden ships, buildings, bridges, and furniture. During the Iron Age, civilizations and trade grew.

How do we get iron? First, we look for iron *ore* in the earth. Iron ore is iron combined with other metals and oxygen. Red iron ore has the most iron. The ore is heated in a *blast furnace*—a furnace that is shaped like a very big smokestack. *Coke*—purified coal—is burned at the bottom of the furnace. Then crushed iron ore mixed with limestone and more coke is dropped down the funnel. The limestone lowers the melting temperature of the ore. The coke reacts with the oxygen in the ore, setting the iron free. The free molten iron is then collected at the bottom of the furnace.

The earth still contains huge reserves of iron ore. There is also plenty of scrap iron that can be remelted and used again. Iron products will continue to be cheaper and more widely used than other metal products.

See also **magnetism; rust;** and **mining.**

Iroquois Indians, *see* Indians, American; Indian Wars

irrigation

Irrigation is a way of watering land. It brings water to places that do not get enough rain to grow crops. Irrigation has been used for thousands of years. The earliest civilizations, including the Sumerian and Egyptian civilizations, were based upon irrigation. In fact, some historians think that civilization began when people learned to plan irrigation systems. Today, farmers in many parts of the world still depend on irrigation to water their crops.

More than 400 million acres of the world's land are irrigated. China, India, the United States, Pakistan, and the Soviet Union are among the countries that do a lot of irrigating. Some countries use more water for irrigating than for anything else.

The water for irrigation comes from either above or below the ground. Water above the ground is called *surface water.* It comes from rainfall, streams, and rivers. The water below the ground is stored in air spaces in layers of sand and rock. A body of rock or sand that holds underground water is called an *aquifer.*

There are several ways of irrigating land. For grains, especially rice, the whole field is flooded. More commonly, water in large canals flows into smaller canals and then into ditches between the rows of plants. Some crops are watered by sprinklers. By the trickle method, water flows through plastic tubes that lie between the rows of plants. Holes all along the tubes let a small amount of water trickle out.

Irrigating land for a long time causes problems. Many underground aquifers are slowly running out of water. Surface water can be used up, too. For example, many irrigation projects draw water from the Colorado River as it flows from the Rocky Mountains to the

An irrigation ditch carries water from a river or reservoir to crops in the fields. At left, a farmer uses an underground sprinkler system to spray water on a crop.

To escape his wife's scolding (left), Rip Van Winkle goes wandering. He is bewitched and sleeps for 20 years. When he wakes up, his house and family are gone (right).

Gulf of California. There is so little water left in the Colorado River that the farmers of Arizona, California, and northern Mexico fight over the water.

Another problem of irrigation is salt. All soils contain some salt. But irrigation may cause salt to collect near the surface. Salt can damage crops and ruin the soil. This may have led to the end of some civilizations that depended on irrigation.

See also farming.

Irving, Washington

Washington Irving was one of the first American writers to win praise in Europe as well as in the U.S. Until then, critics in England and the rest of Europe thought Americans had nothing to write about. Irving showed them they were wrong.

Irving was born in New York City, in 1783. He was the youngest of 11 children. He became a lawyer, but his real love was writing. In 1809, he published his first book, *The History of New York*, which poked fun at New York society. He made up a character, Diedrich Knickerbocker, and pretended Knickerbocker wrote the book. The book was very popular, and the name Knickerbocker came to stand for all New Yorkers. Today, New York's basketball team is called the Knickerbockers, or the "Knicks."

Irving's most famous book was *The Sketch Book*, a collection of short stories and essays. In it are two stories you may be familiar with—"Rip Van Winkle" and "The Legend of Sleepy Hollow."

"Rip Van Winkle" is about a man who goes walking in the Catskill Mountains, in upstate New York. There he meets a strange little man who introduces him to other little men playing ninepins—an early form of bowling. He drinks their liquor and falls asleep. When he wakes up, he learns that he has been asleep for 20 years. His wife is dead. The town no longer remembers him. He is an old man. Fortunately, his daughter is kind and takes the old man in. People grow to love him.

"The Legend of Sleepy Hollow" tells the story of a young schoolteacher named Ichabod Crane. Crane and his friend Brom Bones are both in love with the same girl. One evening, they are at the girl's house telling ghost stories. One scary tale is about the Headless Horseman. Later, as Crane is riding home, this headless ghost chases after him. Poor Ichabod is so terrified that he leaves the town forever. Since Brom Bones ends up marrying the girl, we suspect he was the "ghost" who scared Ichabod away.

Washington Irving died in 1859. Many later writers imitated his comic style of writing. He is still a favorite storyteller.

Nomad boys in North Africa study parts of the Koran written on wood. The Koran is Islam's scripture and was first written in the Arabic language (right).

Islam

Islam is the religion that was founded in Arabia by a man named Muhammad. People who follow the teachings of Muhammad are called *Muslims.* The word *Muslim* means "one who gives himself to Allah." *Allah* is the Islamic word for God.

Muhammad lived from about 570 until 632. As a young man, he worked as a shepherd and a merchant. When he was about 40 years old, he began preaching to the people in the Arabian city of Mecca, where he was born. He said that Allah was the only God and that he was Allah's messenger.

Muhammad was a great soldier. He led Muslim armies into battle to capture cities and territory. Muhammad believed that his victories were victories for Allah. All of Arabia came under the power of Islam during Muhammad's life. (*See* **Muhammad.**)

Islam continued to grow and spread after Muhammad's death. Sometimes, the religion was brought by conquering Muslim armies. At other times, it was spread by merchants and missionaries. Not long after the year 632, Egypt, Syria, and Iraq became Muslim.

Then Muslim armies and teachings spread throughout northern Africa, Spain, Sicily, and southern Italy. In just one hundred years, Islam had become a world religion, and a powerful military force.

Muslims believe that Allah told Muhammad what to teach. His followers wrote down his teachings in a book called the Koran. Muslims respect the Koran the way Jews and Christians respect the Bible. The Koran teaches Muslims who Allah is and how he wants them to live. (*See* **Koran.**)

To live a good life, a Muslim must do five things, called the "five pillars of faith." Just as a pillar supports a building, these five duties are the supports of Islam.

The first pillar is faith. Every Muslim must believe, and say often, "There is no God but Allah, and Muhammad is his Messenger."

The second pillar is daily prayer. Every Muslim must pray five times a day. Muslims may pray at home or in their temples, which are called *mosques.* In places where many Muslims live together, they are called to prayer by a man called a *muezzin.* He climbs onto a high tower—a *minaret*—and chants a special song.

Muslims bow toward Mecca when they pray (right). Many visit the city (above). The black building is the Kaaba, the holiest place in Islam.

Muslims wash themselves before they pray. This is to make themselves pure and clean before going to speak with Allah. When they pray, they kneel down and bend over so that their foreheads touch the floor. They face toward the city of Mecca. Mosques have signs pointing out the direction of Mecca.

Muslims, like Jews, believe that people should not try to make pictures or statues of God. Instead, the walls of mosques are often decorated with colorful tiles and sayings from the Koran.

The Muslim special day of prayer begins each Friday at noon. When the muezzin calls, people gather together in the mosque. There are no priests in Islam, but there are men called *imams* who lead the people in prayer. The imams also teach the people about Allah and about the Muslim way of life.

The third pillar of faith is care for the poor. Muslims give part of what they earn to help support needy neighbors.

The fourth pillar is fasting. A person who is fasting does not eat, or eats very little, for some period of time. Muslims fast for part of

each day during the Islamic month of Ramadan. Ramadan, the ninth month of the Islamic year, is a very strict and serious time in Muslim nations.

The fifth pillar is pilgrimage. *Pilgrimages* are special journeys to places that have religious importance. All Muslims, no matter where they live, are expected to make a pilgrimage to Mecca at least once in their lives.

Islam is a close cousin of Judaism and Christianity. Muhammad taught that Abraham, Moses, Isaiah, and Jesus were all prophets of Allah. But throughout history, Muslims, Christians, and Jews have fought each other.

Muslim armies attacked Christian Europe in the 700s and again in the 1600s. Christian soldiers, called *crusaders,* invaded Muslim lands between the years 1096 and 1291. Muslims and Jews have been fighting in the Middle East for many years. These three groups are still looking for ways to live together peacefully.

There are large Muslim communities today in the Arab states of the Middle East, in India and Pakistan, in Indonesia, in the Soviet Union, and in most African countries.

island

An island is a body of land completely surrounded by water. You may think of continents as islands. But islands are smaller than continents. Also, only two continents—Australia and Antarctica—are *completely* surrounded by water.

Some of the largest islands—Greenland, Britain, and Madagascar—are pieces of land that became separated from continents. Some rocky islands near continental shores were parts of continents at one time. But most islands do not come from continents.

Barrier islands form along the shore of a continent where the water is relatively shallow. Waves and currents keep the sandy seafloor stirred up. They pick up sand from one place and deposit it in another. This builds up long, narrow islands of sand just a few miles offshore and parallel to the coastline. There are barrier islands along the eastern coast of North America.

Islands also form in the deep oceans, far from the continents. The Philippines, a group of islands in the Pacific Ocean, are part of an underwater mountain range. The Hawaiian Islands, Samoan Islands, and Polynesian Islands, also in the Pacific, began as volcanoes rising from the seafloor.

The seafloor is dotted with thousands of volcanoes, many more than there are on land. Many of these volcanoes grow so high that their tops rise above the water. Volcanoes form two kinds of islands—high islands and low islands.

The Hawaiian Islands are high islands. They were formed by a chain of volcanoes. Only Hawaii, the island at the eastern end of the chain, still has active volcanoes. The volcanoes that formed the other islands are *extinct*—they no longer erupt.

Low islands develop from volcanoes that do not rise very high above the ocean surface. Coral likes to grow around the sides of volcanoes. New corals grow on the skeletons of dead corals. A huge mass of coral builds up as the volcano sinks, until there is an island, called an *atoll*. Because atolls grow around the sunken volcano, they are shaped like rings. They have shallow seawater *lagoons* in their centers. (*See* **coral** and **reef.**)

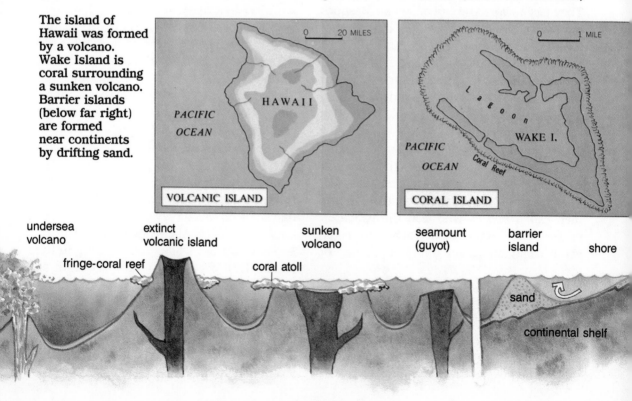

The island of Hawaii was formed by a volcano. Wake Island is coral surrounding a sunken volcano. Barrier islands (below far right) are formed near continents by drifting sand.

0   20 MILES

PACIFIC OCEAN

HAWAII

VOLCANIC ISLAND

0   1 MILE

Lagoon

PACIFIC OCEAN

Coral Reef

WAKE I.

CORAL ISLAND

undersea volcano

extinct volcanic island

sunken volcano

seamount (guyot)

barrier island

shore

fringe-coral reef

coral atoll

sand

continental shelf

Israel

Capital: Jerusalem
Area: 7,847 square miles (20,324 square kilometers)
Population (1985): 4,128,000
Official languages: Hebrew and Arabic

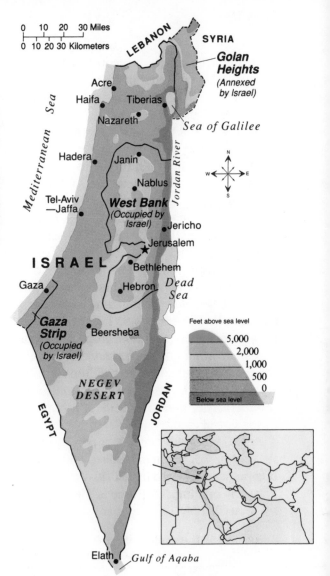

Israel is a small Middle Eastern country on the eastern shore of the Mediterranean Sea. It is different from most other countries, because it was formed by the United Nations in 1948 as a country for Jews. After 1948, hundreds of thousands of Jews came to Israel from many parts of the world. One of Israel's presidents, Golda Meir, came to Israel from the United States.

The lands of Israel are very special to the Jewish people. Today's Jews are descendants of the people who lived in this region more than 3,000 years ago. The early Jews—the Israelites—built a strong kingdom. They also built a great temple to God at Jerusalem (*See* **Israelites.**)

Israel is also special to Christians. Christians call the area the Holy Land. It is where Jesus was born and lived. His followers began the Christian religion. About 600 years later, the prophet Muhammad began the Islamic religion in nearby Arabia. Muhammad made a visit to Jerusalem, so a part of Israel is special to Muslims, too.

Land Israel has about as much land as the state of New Jersey. Most of Israel is very dry. In fact, the Negev Desert, which covers much of the country's southern half, is one of the world's driest places. Parts of the Negev receive less than 1 inch (2.5 centimeters) of rain a year.

On the eastern edge of the Negev Desert is the Dead Sea. It got its name because it is so salty that plants and fish cannot live in it. The shore of the Dead Sea is more than 1,300 feet (396 meters) below sea level. That makes the Dead Sea shore the lowest land on Earth. (*See* **Dead Sea.**)

Much of central Israel is open plain. It gets little rain, yet is still a productive farming region. Israeli farmers irrigate their crops by bringing water from other parts of the country through man-made waterways. The dry climate is very good for growing citrus fruit, Israel's main export crop.

One of the few rainy spots in Israel is in the north. This is a land of hills and mountains with lush, green valleys.

People Israel is the most advanced country in the Middle East. Its many schools, factories, hospitals, and apartment buildings are all modern and well equipped.

Most Israelis live in the central part of the country. The two most important cities are Jerusalem and Tel Aviv. Jerusalem, to the east, is the capital. Tel Aviv, on the Mediterranean Sea, is Israel's main port and center of business and industry.

About eight out of ten people in Israel are Jews. Many of the non-Jews are Arab Palestinians whose families lived on the land before Israel was made a country. Most of them live apart from their Jewish neighbors, in Arab communities.

Much of Israeli life centers around Jewish customs and traditions. This is especially true on a *kibbutz.* Kibbutzim are farming communities where people live as a group. Kibbutz members share the crops they grow and share other goods and services, too. On some kibbutzim, all the children live together. They are raised according to Jewish tradition. There are hundreds of kibbutzim in the Israeli countryside.

Jewish traditions are also a part of life in the cities. For example, most stores and businesses are closed from Friday evening to Saturday evening. This time is the Sabbath, the Jewish holy day. In many restaurants

Jerusalem is the capital of Israel. The walls of the old city are in the distance.

and government buildings, only *kosher* food is served. Kosher food is prepared according to the rules of Jewish tradition.

History Around A.D. 100, the early Jewish people were driven out of Israel and scattered to many different countries. Even though they did not have their own country, they kept their religion alive.

In the late 1800s, a few of them began returning to the Middle East. By then, the old land of Israel had a new name—Palestine. The returning Jews, called *Zionists,* hoped to set up a new country for Jews from around the world. In 1947, the United Nations set up such a country, and in 1948, Israel was born.

Many of Israel's neighbors are Arab countries. Their people are Muslims. They were very angry when the United Nations set aside land for Israel. Since 1948, there have been several wars and many smaller battles between Israel and its neighbors. Because of the wars, every 18-year-old boy and girl in Israel must serve in the armed forces for two years.

In 1979, President Carter of the United States met with Menachem Begin, the leader of Israel, and Anwar el-Sadat, the leader of Egypt. With Carter's help, they agreed to sign a treaty to end years of war between their two countries. But Israel and its other neighbors have continued to quarrel.

Israelites

The Israelites were the Jews of ancient times. Most of our knowledge of them comes from the Hebrew Bible, also known as the Old Testament. To find out about their religious beliefs and practices, *see* **Judaism.**

According to tradition, Jewish history began with three men known as *patriarchs.* They were Abraham, his son Isaac, and his grandson Jacob. They lived in the land of Canaan, the region of western Asia that was later called Palestine. Jacob had 12 sons, each of whom led a tribe. Since Jacob was also known as Israel, the members of the 12

Moses, an Israelite leader, brought the
Ten Commandments down from a mountain (above).
They told how God wanted people to live.
The Israelites settled in the land of Canaan (left).

tribes became known as the children of Israel, or Israelites. (*See* **Abraham.**)

Many Israelites moved to Egypt. One of them, Joseph, became a trusted adviser to the Egyptian king, called the *pharaoh.* But one of the pharaohs enslaved the Jews. Finally, an Israelite leader named Moses led his people out of Egypt. This movement is known as the Exodus. Historians believe it happened during the 1200s B.C.—over 3,000 years ago.

For 40 years, Moses and his people wandered in the desert. During that time, God appeared to Moses and presented him with the Ten Commandments. Finally, after Moses died, his people returned to Canaan, the "promised land." (*See* **Moses.**)

At first, all the Israelites lived under one ruler—first Saul, then David, and then Solomon. The Israelites built a great temple to God in Jerusalem. (*See* **David.**)

After Solomon died, the Israelites split into two kingdoms. Ten of their tribes lived in the kingdom of Israel, in the north. The other two tribes lived in the kingdom of Judah, in the south. Jerusalem was its capital. The word *Jew* comes from the name Judah.

The small Israelite kingdoms were no match for the stronger powers of western Asia. In the 700s B.C., the Assyrians conquered Israel. Most of the ten northern tribes became mixed with the other peoples of the region. They are often called the "ten lost tribes of Israel."

Judah, too, was conquered—first by the Assyrians, then by the Egyptians. Early in the 500s B.C., the Babylonians defeated Judah, destroyed the Temple, and took most of the Jews captive. But the descendants of the captives returned to Jerusalem and rebuilt the Temple.

For many years, the Israelites of Jerusalem were allowed to live in peace. Then, in the 100s B.C., they clashed with the Syrians, who controlled this area. The Syrian ruler wanted the Jews to give up their religion.

When they refused, he attacked them. The Jews resisted. Led by a man named Judah Maccabee, they defeated the Syrians. They managed to remain independent for about 100 years.

The Jews quarreled among themselves, however. This made it easy for the Romans to defeat them and rule them. The Jews revolted, but the Roman Empire was too strong for them. In A.D. 70, the Romans conquered Jerusalem, and the Temple was destroyed again.

Even before the Roman conquest, Jews had begun to move to other regions of Asia and to North Africa and Europe. Afterward, this movement grew. The Jews were often treated badly by the people they lived among. (*See* **Hitler, Adolf.**)

But Jews never lost their identity or their pride in their history. Many dreamed of returning to their ancient homeland. Finally, in 1948, the United Nations created a new nation for Jews—Israel. (*See* **Israel.**)

isthmus

An isthmus is a narrow strip of land that is like a bridge between two large land areas. An isthmus usually separates two seas or two oceans from each other. That is why an isthmus is a good place to cut a canal for ships. A canal through an isthmus makes a

The arrow points to an isthmus—a "neck" of land between Cape Cod and the mainland.

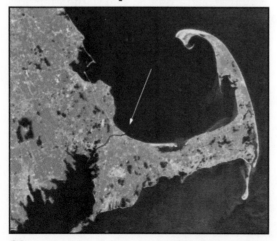

shortcut for ships traveling from one ocean to another.

The Isthmus of Suez is a narrow strip of land joining Africa and Asia, and separating the Mediterranean and Red seas. Ancient Egyptians built canals across the isthmus to connect the Red Sea with the Nile River. The present-day Suez Canal was dug across this isthmus during a ten-year period—from 1859 to 1869.

The Isthmus of Panama connects two other continents—North America and South America. It also separates the Atlantic Ocean from the Pacific. The 65-kilometer (40-mile) Panama Canal cuts across this long, narrow neck of land.

See also **canal.**

Italy

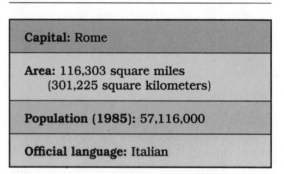

Capital: Rome
Area: 116,303 square miles (301,225 square kilometers)
Population (1985): 57,116,000
Official language: Italian

Italy is a country in southern Europe. The northern part borders France, Switzerland, Austria, and Yugoslavia. The rest of the country is a peninsula that reaches south into the Mediterranean Sea. On a map, Italy looks like a huge high-heeled boot. The country also includes two large islands —Sicily and Sardinia.

Land If you visit Italy, you soon see that much of the country is hilly or mountainous. The highest mountains are the Alps, which run along Italy's northern border. Many of the peaks are more than 10,000 feet (3,000 meters) high. (*See* **Alps.**)

The Apennine Mountains run almost all the way down the Italian peninsula. They are not as high as the Alps, but they are very rugged mountains.

SWITZERLAND

AUSTRIA

A L P S

FRANCE

Lake Maggiore

Lake Como

Bolzano

Turin

Milan

Lake Garda

Verona

Padua

Trieste

Brescia

Adige River

Venice

Po River

YUGOSLAVIA

Genoa

Parma

Ferrara

ELEVATION
Feet
Over 10000
5000 — 10000
2000 — 5000
1000 — 2000
0 — 1000

0   MILES   100

La Spezia

Modena

Bologna

SAN MARINO

Pisa

Livorno

Florence

Ancona

Ligurian Sea

Elba

Perugia

APPENINE MOUNTAINS

Adriatic Sea

N
W   E
S

Corsica (Fr.)

Tiber River

VATICAN CITY

★ Rome

I T A L Y

Sassari

Foggia

Sardinia

Naples

Vesuvius (Vol.)

Bari

This huge
statue
is part of
an outdoor
fountain
in Rome.

Tyrrhenian Sea

Ischia

Pompeii Ruins

Capri

Taranto

Brindisi

Cagliari

Gulf of Taranto

Palermo

Messina

Reggio di Calabria

Sicily

Catania

M e d i t e r r a n e a n   S e a

The most important farming areas are in
the north, where there is more rain. The Po
River valley is a major farming center.
Wheat, corn, sugar beets, and flax for cloth-
making are the main crops. Southern Italy is
rugged and receives little rain, so it is difficult to grow crops there. Two crops that will
grow in many parts of the country are olives
and grapes. Some of the oil from the olives is
used for cooking, and the rest is exported. A
lot of the grapes are made into wine. In fact,
Italy is one of the world's main producers of
wine.

95

People Italy is also an important manufacturing country. Most of its manufacturing is in the northern cities of Milan, Turin, and Genoa. Italian factories make automobiles, tractors, chemicals, and cloth.

Italy welcomes millions of visitors every year. People come to ski in the Italian Alps or relax on the warm beaches of the Mediterranean Sea in the south. Many come to visit famous ancient cities and to see the great art in Italian museums. The beautiful old city of Venice is especially interesting—most of its "streets" are canals.

Opera—a kind of stage play that is sung instead of spoken—is very special to Italians. Many of the great operas of the world are in the Italian language, and many of the great opera composers were Italian. La Scala in Milan is the world's most famous opera house. (*See* **opera** and **composers**.)

Most Italians are Roman Catholics. The world center of that church is in Vatican City, a tiny independent country that is surrounded by the city of Rome.

The cathedral in Florence is one of many inspiring churches in Italy.

History For many centuries, the Romans were the most powerful people in the ancient world. They built a huge empire that covered all of Italy and most of the lands surrounding the Mediterranean Sea as well. (*See* **Roman Empire.**)

In the late 400s, invaders from the north conquered most of Italy, and the Roman Empire ended. Different governments controlled parts of Italy. The larger cities—such as Florence, Genoa, and Venice—became important countries all by themselves.

Beginning in the 1300s, a movement called the *Renaissance*—"rebirth"—began in Italy. Artists and writers began to imitate ancient Roman and Greek art. Often, they used this art to decorate churches and other buildings. Michelangelo, Leonardo da Vinci, and other great artists made Italy famous. (*See* **Renaissance; Michelangelo;** and **Leonardo da Vinci.**)

Until 1861, present-day Italy was still made up of many small countries. Then a group of Italian patriots brought nearly all of Italy together under one king.

In the late 1800s and early 1900s, thousands of Italians left Italy and came to the United States to live. Today, there are millions of Italian Americans.

In the 1920s, Benito Mussolini became a powerful leader in Italy. In the 1930s, Italian armies invaded Ethiopia. Mussolini joined with the German leader Adolf Hitler to fight the Allies—France, Britain, and the Soviet Union—in World War II. The United States joined the Allies in 1941, and American and British troops invaded Italy. Mussolini was captured and killed, and Italy surrendered in 1943. (*See* **World War II.**)

Since World War II, Italy has had a parliamentary form of government. Italy is a member of the European Economic Community, which is also called the Common Market. Italy trades with many countries in Europe and around the world.

Ivory Coast, *see* **Africa**